SMART INVESTING

B/W EDITION

SMART INVESTING

How to Invest Money and be Your own Money Manager!

B/W EDITION

By

Ray Gazelle, CFP®

Gazelle Financial Publishing

Gazelle Financial Publishing

Edgewater, Maryland

ISBN13: 9780998704609

CONTENTS

PREFACE

The purpose of "Smart Investing" is to focus on the mechanics and principles of investing one's money.

To end up where you want to be, an investor needs a roadmap, a financial plan.

As a Certified Financial Planner™ professional (CFP®), I realized working with clients that what clients needed the most was an organized plan to invest their money. Most people have developed skills and knowledge about their particular business that have helped make them successful. They have the intellect to differentiate good investments from bad ones. What is needed is a game plan or road map to get there, i.e. the sequence of steps to build a comprehensive investing plan.

Detailed information is provided in a format that walks the reader through the process to assess one's risk tolerance, set an allocation strategy, define an investment policy and pick funds appropriate for a particular investment risk tolerance and horizon.

As a potential investor reads on, what he or she realizes is that each section is a building block that is developing an investment plan and ultimately the methods and procedures for investing one's money. It is my objective to have laid out principles of investing so that applied properly, an investor will be ready to select the appropriate investment vehicles in the right quantities for their risk tolerance and stage of life.

Essentially, to provide a roadmap and discipline for investing money – a do-it-yourself guidebook to investing.

INTRODUCTION

Knowing how to secure your financial well-being is one of the most important things you'll ever need in life. You gain control over your daily finances and the ability to make choices based on what you want and need.

Time after time, people of varying means begin the journey to reach their goals; whether that is buying a home, education opportunities for their children, or a comfortable retirement. Most people attain financial security by saving and investing over a long period of time. The sooner one starts the better; however, it's never too late to start.

Every successful investor starts with the basic principles and develops an investing strategy. It requires the development of certain skills and knowledge that may or may not be similar to one's vocation. However unfamiliar any of this may seem, the basics are rather easy to learn. The most important tools, your intellect, you already have.

"Smart Investing" starts with the process of setting goals and getting acquainted with your financial position, i.e. what is your net worth and how do you make and spend money. This will help to organize your thoughts and focus on the important matters in your financial life.

The next and very important step is assessing one's risk tolerance. This is one of the most critical aspects of investing. It will guide the whole process and if done properly, it will let you sleep at night and maintain your investing resolve through the good and bad times.

Next, the components of the investing world are explained, including the products: stock, bonds, mutual funds, etc.; and the players: brokers, financial professionals and rating agencies.

Also, a brief review of the dynamics of the world we live in is presented, i.e. the economics of the business cycle.

Continuing with the process of building a plan, one's asset allocation to risk assets and fixed income is assessed and determined based on individual risk tolerance and time horizon. Then this basic asset allocation is diversified into sub-asset classes for the purpose of mitigating risk. We learn how asset classes are correlated and how this relationship has affected them over time and through major crises.

Putting it all together, model portfolios of mutual funds and exchange traded funds (ETF's) are presented as an examples of how to build a diversified portfolio with less than ten funds.

As a final step an investment policy is written for one's individual situation that is the roadmap or guidelines for investing. It will include the chosen risk tolerance, investment strategy, asset allocation ranges, investment choices, asset quality requirements and one's current target asset allocations.

"Smart Investing's" objective is to prepare a potential investor to understand the processes necessary to select appropriate investment vehicles and in the right quantities for their unique situation and to be ready to invest money.

Let's get started!

To begin setting the course for your financial future, you need to know where you are going and why – The Goals. And, what are the resources to begin getting you there – The Financial Position. It's an important starting point.

The steps in the next chapter take you through the process to document your Goals and Financial Position.

I
FINANCIAL GOALS & POSITION

Define Your Goals:

Ask yourself what are my most important goals, i.e. things or events that you want to save and invest to obtain. Here are some possibilities:

A home	A car or boat
Education	A comfortable retirement
Children	Paying of debt
An Emergency fund	Medical or other emergencies
Caring for parents	Vacation Home

Make a list and then think about which goals are the most important. List the most important goals first. How much money will be needed? By when, i.e. how many years?

Personal Financial Goals	How Much ($)	By When
1. _____	_____	_____
2. _____	_____	_____
3. _____	_____	_____
4. _____	_____	_____
5. _____	_____	_____

Many tools exist to help decide how much will need to be saved for various needs.

- Retirement: For example, the Ballpark Estimate, a single-page worksheet created by the American Savings Education Council, can help calculate what one needs to save each year for retirement. Other organizations including Charles Schwab, Kiplinger, Vanguard and Fidelity (to name a few) have calculators that vary in complexity.
- College Savings: The Financial Industry Regulatory Authority (FINRA) has a college savings calculator. Most mutual fund and brokerage companies such as Fidelity, T Rowe Price and Charles Schwab also have college savings calculators.
- Social Security: The Social Security Administration has a benefits calculator to estimate potential benefit amounts.

What is My Current Financial Situation?

Let's take an honest look at your financial situation. Ask yourself: what do I own and what do I owe? You'll be creating a "net worth statement." The first section, what is owned, is one's "assets". The second section, what is owed other people, are "liabilities" or debts.

The next page contains a worksheet for this purpose.

ASSETS	Current Value	Notes and Comments
Cash and Bank Checking Accounts		
Savings and C.D.'s		
Annuities		
Investments: Mutual Funds & Brokerage Accounts		
IRA'S and Retirement Accounts		
U.S. Treasury Bonds EE, etc.		
Vested Pension Value		
Deferred Compensation		
Retirement Severance Pay		
Real Estate - Primary Residence		
Real Estate - Other (Attach a list)		
Automobiles		
Life Insurance Cash Value		
Other Liquid Assets		
Other Illiquid Assets		
TOTAL ASSETS		

LIABILITIES	Current Value	Notes and Comments
Credit Card Debt		
Auto Loan(s)		
Other Short-Term Debt		
Mortgage Loan - Primary Residence		
Mortgage Loan(s) - Other		
Equity Loan/Line		
Other Long-Term Debt		
Other Obligations		
TOTAL LIABILITIES		
NET WORTH		

Calculating Net Worth

Complete the worksheet above filling in the various items that are appropriate to your situation. After completing the sections, then total the two sections, Assets and Liabilities.

Subtract the liabilities from the assets to obtain the "Net Worth" total. If the assets are larger than the liabilities, there is a "positive" net worth. If the liabilities are greater than the assets, then the net worth is "negative".

A positive net worth is where you want to be. If you have a negative net worth, getting into a positive position is an important financial priority and the right thing to do for your financial future. It should be one of the goals on the goal list, making it part of the long term financial planning.

The "net worth statement" should be updated every year to keep track of its status.

KNOW YOUR INCOME AND EXPENSES

Determining where all your income comes from and how it is then spent or used creates a *"personal cash flow statement"*. This exercise requires documenting the monthly or annual income and expense items in a particular format.

The *Income section* is what is earned by members of the family. *Expenses* are separated into Discretionary and Non-discretionary. The Non-discretionary Expenses are expenses that one is obligated to pay such as a mortgage payment, car payment or utility bill. The Discretionary Expenses are the ones that are not essential, where there is a choice on whether to spend the money or not. This category is where the opportunity lies to generate additional money to save or pay down debt.

The bottom line (Net = Income minus Expenses) is the money left over for additional savings or for other financial purposes.

The following worksheet is provided to assist in developing a cash flow statement.

INCOME	Monthly Amount	Annual Total	Notes and Comments
Div. & Int. Income			
Other Invest Inc.			
Alimony Received			
Other Income			
Salary 1			
Salary 2			
Social Security 1			
Social Security 2			
Pension 1			
Pension 2			
Net Business Inc.			
Total income:			

EXPENSES	Monthly Amount	Annual Total	Notes and Comments
Non-Discretionary:			
Mortgage - Principal/Interest			Rate: Maturity Date: Balance:
Mortgage - Taxes			
Mortgage - Hazard Insurance			
Home Equity Loan			
Rent			
HOA Dues			
Auto Insurance			
Auto Loan			
Alimony Paid			
Child Care			
Child Support			
Clothing			
Groceries			
Health Care			
Doctor			
Medicine			
Dentist			
Vision			
Insurance			
Life Insurance			
Long Term Care Ins			
Umbrella Insurance			
Professional Fees & Licenses			
Utilities			
Electric			
Gas			
Cable			
Telephone & Cellular			
Trash Removal			
Water/Sewer			
Other Loans/Debt.			
Total Non-Discretionary			

Discretionary Expenses:	Monthly Amount	Annual Total	Notes and Comments
VISA, MC & Am Express			
Auto Gasoline, oil, etc.			
Auto Maintenance			
Charity			
Contrib. Other			
Dining/Entertain			
Dry Cleaning			
Gifts (Birthday, Holiday)			
Home Maintenance/Landscape			
Household			
Misc./Other			
Personal Care (Hair, etc.)			
Professional non-reimbursed			
Recreation			
Savings			
Savings: 401K/403B/TSA			
Subscriptions			
Tax Preparation Fee			
Vacation/Travel			
Auto Replacement Escrow			
Total Discretionary			
Total Expenses:			
Tax: Federal			
Tax: State			
Tax: FICA/Medicare			
Tax: Personal Property			
Tax: Business			
Grand Total Exp.:			
NET: INCOME - EXPENSES			

At this point a great amount of work has been done getting to know your financial position and what financial goals are important. The groundwork has been done collecting important information that will help make decisions for a financial plan.

In summary,

- Personal financial goals should be listed including the amount of money needed and the timeframe.
- One's net worth, the amount of money or asset value greater than the money owed to others.
- The amount of money that is being saved on a regular basis and the amount of net income available for additional savings or other financial purposes.

The next step will be to determine Risk Tolerance.

II
RISK TOLERANCE

Determine Your Risk Tolerance

When one "invests" money, there is a greater chance of losing money than when one "saves". Unlike FDIC-insured deposits, the money invested in securities, mutual funds, and other similar investments are not federally insured. You could lose your "principal," which is the amount you've invested. That's true even if investments are purchased through a bank. But investing also has the opportunity to earn more money than savings.

But what about risk? All investments involve taking on risk. It's important to fully understand that investment in stocks, bonds or mutual funds could lose some or all of the money invested in any one investment. While over the long term the stock market has historically provided around 10% annual returns (closer to 6% or 7% "real" returns when the effects of inflation are subtracted), the long term does sometimes take a rather long, long time to play out. Those who invested all of their money in the stock market at its peak in 1929 (before the stock market crash) would wait over 20 years to see the stock market return to the same level.

Consider the market (S&P 500) fluctuations since the new millennium:

- The market peaked in March 2000 at 1527, then declined to 777 by October 2002
- Peaked again in October 2007 at 1565, then declined to 677 by March 2009
- Peaked again in July 2015 at 2130

How much risk should you assume?

Categories of risk may have labels such as "income", "moderate", "growth," or "aggressive growth." Be certain to fully understand the distinctions among these terms, and be certain that the risk level chosen accurately reflects age, experience, timeframe and investment goals. The investment products chosen must reflect the category of risk that has been selected.

The following sets of questions are designed to help work through the process of determining individual "risk tolerance".

Complete the following two sets of questions:

INVESTMENT OBJECTIVES:

What are your investment objectives? As an overall categorization of your investment objectives, please select ONE of the following statements that most accurately represents those objectives:

1. *Safety of principal is my primary concern. The amount of capital appreciation and income my investments earn are secondary objectives.*

2. *My investments should be relatively safe and emphasize current income.*

3. *My investments may be exposed to moderate levels of risk with the primary goal of generating current income. Capital appreciation over time is a secondary objective.*

4. *My investments may be exposed to risk and should emphasize growth over time, but should also generate some current income.*

5. *My investments should emphasize 100% growth over the long term and can be exposed to the full risk that accompanies a diversified equity portfolio.*

6. *Other: Please specify,*

_____

RISK TOLERANCE AND EXPERIENCE

The following questions are intended to help measure your attitude toward investment risk as it applies to your financial goals.

	Strongly Agree	Agree	Disagree	Strongly Disagree
I am prepared to sacrifice some safety in exchange for higher returns.	O	O	O	O
I am willing to accept some risk in effort to stay ahead of inflation.	O	O	O	O
From time to time, I can tolerate negative returns.	O	O	O	O
I am willing to take above average risks to achieve above average returns.	O	O	O	O

After answering the two sets of questions above, look over the risk tolerance definitions on the next page and select the one that most closely matches your personal feelings about risk taking when investing money.

Risk Tolerance Classification Definitions

Risk Tolerance: Select one of the six Risk Tolerance classifications, as defined below, based on responses to the above *questions.*

Also, consider the timeframe and experience investing money. Your risk tolerance should reflect the amount of risk you are comfortable taking or accepting when investing money. It is important to recognize when there are material changes in your financial condition or risk tolerance.

1. CONSERVATIVE: A Conservative investor values protecting principal over seeking appreciation. This investor is comfortable accepting lower returns for a higher degree of liquidity and/or stability. Typically, a Conservative investor primarily seeks to minimize risk and loss of principal.

2. MODERATELY CONSERVATIVE: A Moderately Conservative investor values principal preservation, but is comfortable accepting a small degree of risk and volatility to seek some degree of appreciation. This investor desires greater liquidity, is willing to accept lower returns, and is willing to accept minimal losses.

3. MODERATE: A Moderate investor values reducing risks and enhancing returns equally. This investor is willing to accept modest risks to seek higher long-term returns. A Moderate investor may endure a short-term loss of principal and lower degree of liquidity in exchange for long-term appreciation.

4. MODERATE GROWTH: A Moderate Growth investor values higher long-term returns and is willing to accept considerable risk. This investor is comfortable with short-term fluctuations in exchange for seeking long-term appreciation. The Moderate Growth investor is willing to endure larger short-term losses of principal in exchange for the potential of higher long-term returns. Liquidity is a secondary concern to a Moderate Growth investor.

5. MODERATELY AGGRESSIVE: A Moderately Aggressive investor primarily values higher long-term returns and is willing to accept significant risk. This investor believes higher long-term returns are more important than protecting principal. A Moderately Aggressive investor may endure large losses in favor of potentially higher long-term returns. Liquidity may not be a concern to a Moderately Aggressive investor.

6. AGGRESSIVE: An Aggressive investor values maximizing returns and is willing to accept substantial risk. This investor believes maximizing long-term returns is more important than protecting principal. An Aggressive investor may endure extensive volatility and significant losses. Liquidity is generally not a concern to an Aggressive investor.

The next few chapters will review Investment Choices, Rating Agencies and Business Cycles.

III
STOCKS, BONDS vs. FUNDS

Investment Products: What are the Choices?

When making an investment, an investor is giving money to a company or an enterprise, hoping that it will be successful and be paid back with even more money.

Some investments make money, and some don't. Money may potentially be made in an investment if:
- The company performs better than its competitors.
- Other investors recognize it's a good company, so that when it comes time to sell the investment, others want to buy it.
- The company makes profits, meaning they make enough money to pay interest for their bonds issued, or maybe dividends on the stock.

Stocks

When investing in a stock, an investor buys ownership shares in a company—also known as equity shares. The return on investment is the amount that is returned to the investor compared to what is put in or invested; and depends on the success or failure of the company. If the company does well and makes money from the products or services it sells, the investor expects to benefit from that success. There are two main ways to make money with stocks:

1. **Dividends.** When publicly owned companies are profitable, they can choose to distribute some of those earnings to shareholders by paying a dividend. Dividends may either be taken in cash or reinvested to purchase more shares in the company. Many retired investors focus on stocks that generate regular dividend income to replace income they no longer receive from their jobs. Stocks that

pay a higher than average dividend are sometimes referred to as "income stocks."

2. **Capital gains.** Stocks are bought and sold constantly throughout each trading day, and their prices change all the time. When a stock price goes higher than what was paid to buy it, shares may be sold at a profit. These profits are known as capital gains. In contrast, if the stock is sold for a lower price than originally paid to buy it, a capital loss is incurred.

Both dividends and capital gains depend on the fortunes of the company—dividends are paid from the company's earnings and capital gains are based on investor demand for the stock. Demand normally reflects the prospects for the company's future performance. Strong demand—the result of many investors wanting to buy a particular stock—tends to result in an increase in the stock's share price. Conversely, if the company isn't profitable or if investors are selling rather than buying its stock, the shares may be worth less than originally paid for them.

The performance of an individual stock is also affected by what's happening in the stock market in general, which is in turn affected by the economy as a whole. For example, if interest rates go up and investors think they may make more money with bonds than with stock, they might sell off stock and use that money to buy bonds. If many investors feel the same way, the stock market as a whole is likely to drop in value, which in turn may affect the value of the investments investors hold. Other factors, such as political uncertainty, energy or weather problems, or corporate profits, also influence market performance.

However, and this is an important element of investing, at a certain point stock prices will be low enough to attract investors again. If investors begin to buy, stock prices tend to rise, offering the potential for making a profit. That expectation may breathe new life into the stock market as more people invest.

This cyclical pattern, specifically the pattern of strength and weakness in the stock market and the majority of stocks that trade in the stock market recurs continually; though the schedule isn't predictable. Sometimes, the market moves from strength to weakness and back to strength in only a few months. Other times, this movement, which is known as a full market cycle, takes years. Market cycles are covered in more detail in a subsequent chapter.

Because it is sometimes hard for investors to become experts on various businesses, for example, what are the best steel, automobile, or telephone companies; investors often depend on professionals who are trained to research companies and recommend companies that are likely to succeed.

Since it takes work to pick the stocks or bonds of the companies that have the best chance to do well in the future, many investors choose to invest in mutual funds.

Mutual Funds

What is a mutual fund?

A mutual fund is a pool of money run by a professional or group of professionals called the "investment adviser." In a managed mutual fund, after investigating the prospects of many companies, the fund's investment adviser will pick the stocks or bonds of companies and put them into a fund. Investors can buy shares of the fund, and their shares rise or fall in value as the values of the stocks and bonds in the fund rise and fall.

Investors may typically pay a fee when they buy or sell their shares in the fund, and those fees in part pay the salaries and expenses of the professionals who manage the fund.

Even small fees can and do add up and eat into a significant chunk of the returns a mutual fund is likely to produce, so look carefully at how much a fund costs and think about how much it will cost over the investing horizon. If two funds are similar in every way except that one charges a higher fee than the other, more money will be made by choosing the fund with the lower annual costs.

Mutual Funds without Active Management

An Index Fund is a mutual fund that does not attempt to pick and choose stocks of individual companies based upon the research of the mutual fund managers or to try to time the market's movements. An index fund seeks to equal the returns of a major stock index, such as the Standard & Poor 500, the Wilshire 5000, or the Russell 3000. Through computer programmed buying and selling, an index fund tracks the holdings of a chosen index, and so shows the same returns as an index minus, of course, the annual fees involved in running the fund. *The fees for index mutual funds generally are much lower than the fees for managed mutual funds.*

Historical data shows that index funds have, primarily because of their lower fees, enjoyed higher returns than the average managed mutual fund. But, like any investment, index funds involve risk.

Exchange Traded Funds

An Exchange Traded Fund or ETF is a marketable security that tracks an index, a commodity, bonds, or a basket of assets like an index fund. Unlike mutual funds, an ETF trades like a common stock on a stock exchange and therefore may be bought and sold throughout the day; whereas a mutual fund is bought or sold after the market closes. ETFs experience price changes throughout the day just like a stock. ETFs typically have higher daily liquidity and lower fees than mutual fund shares, making them an attractive alternative for individual investors. Lately some ETFs are coming to market that are managed and mimic the traditional mutual fund in that regard.

Let's look more closely at stocks and equity mutual funds.

Stocks vs. Funds

When building an investment portfolio of risk assets, an investor must decide whether to use individual stocks or mutual funds and ETFs. Stocks may be more interesting to some investors because they may get more involved in the business and the "story" that the company has to tell. Mutual funds on the other hand are more of a black box. The managers are building the portfolio and it is unknown at any given time exactly what they are investing in, since they buy and sell some of their holdings almost daily.

Individual stocks. Individual stocks may present more opportunity than many mutual funds. A portfolio of individual stocks is usually more concentrated than a mutual fund, where the performance of an individual security makes a greater impact on the overall portfolio. This concentration brings more risk to the portfolio, therefore it is important for diversification to purchase a minimum of 25 to 50 different stocks in different industries. Consider a portfolio invested evenly across only ten stocks, when one goes belly up, the portfolio would have a big loss if the others did not perform extremely well. Conversely, that same stock could double in value and significantly help the portfolio. Having the expertise to pick the right stocks and at the right time is important to investing success.

Mutual funds. Investing in well-known highly rated Mutual funds, will normally guarantee diversification among many asset classes. The beauty of this approach is that an investor can get into many types of stocks and no single company will break the portfolio. However, because it is so diversified, no individual company will significantly help the portfolio. The result is a smoother ride and hopefully steady returns. The highs will not be as high and the lows will not be as low. Most people like mutual funds for this reason.

Diversification: As mentioned, one of the benefits of mutual funds is that it allows a small investor to invest in a basket of securities all at once. Investors need not worry about picking securities separately. Unlike a concentrated portfolio of individual stocks, underperformance of a single security gets mitigated by outperformance of so many others in the mutual fund portfolio.

Professional Management: Most mutual funds are professionally managed. An exception is a mutual fund or ETF that tracks an index. Investors need not worry about the timing of stock picking and selling since this is the responsibility of the fund manager. Fund managers may also employ various investment strategies with the objective of getting the best returns from a particular market cycle, i.e. Bull or Bear market.

Individual stock investment portfolios may also be professionally managed if the investor has appointed a portfolio manager. In this case appropriate management fees are charged and there may be a large minimum investment required as a prerequisite for the service.

Fees:

Individual Stocks. When individual stocks are bought or sold, the brokerage company charges a transaction fee. This fee for discount brokers is usually $8 to $10 or possibly less. The exchange where the stock is traded charges a small fee for the sale of a stock, usually considerably less than $1.

If the stock portfolio is managed by an appointed portfolio manager, a portfolio management fee may average approximately 1% but charges may range from .5% to 2% depending on the manager and size of the portfolio.

Mutual Funds. In the case of mutual funds, there are many fees, most are hidden and only show up in regulatory disclosures. The following information briefly describes these fees:

- **Sales charges** also known as loads or commissions, apply to any fund that is not a "No Load" fund. There might be a charge for buying into the fund (a front-end load) or selling the fund (back-end load, deferred sales charge, or redemption fee). It is best to avoid all of these. When buying an actively managed fund, buy the fund with no sales charges at all, i.e. "No Load".
- **Expense ratios** represent the annual fees charged by all funds, including the management fee, the administrative costs, 12b-1 distribution fees, and other operating expenses. It is important to make sure that the fees are as low as possible. Index funds typically

charge about 0.20% of the assets or less; and actively managed funds currently average about 1.5% per year and many are higher. Any fund that has fees above 1% per year should be considered very high in expenses.

Turnover: Turnover is a measurement of how long a fund holds on to the stocks in its portfolio. The longer a mutual fund holds on to a stock and the less trading the fund does, the lower the turnover will be. Since a fund incurs costs every time it buys and sells stocks, the lower the turnover, the lower the transaction costs incurred by the fund and usually the lower the capital gains distributed. Funds that have a turnover of 100% are essentially buying a completely new set of companies every year. Turnover should ideally be substantially lower than the mutual fund average of about 80%. Index funds have turnover as low as 5%.

A mutual fund shopping list should read:

- *No sales charges, i.e. "No Load" funds*

- *A low expense ratio (below 1.00%)*

- *Low turnover, no higher than 50% a year, and preferably closer to 20%*

Taxes: Whether stocks or mutual funds, taxes must be paid for dividends and capital gains when the investment is in a taxable, non-retirement account. Regarding tax efficiency, since the investor determines when to buy or sell the holdings, a stock portfolio may be more tax efficient than a mutual fund; an investor has no control over the amount of capital gains distributed by a mutual fund. Portfolio management fees, if charged separately, are tax-deductible. Mutual fund fees are not tax deductible.

Bonds vs. Funds

Bond mutual funds have many of the same pros as stock mutual funds in that buying one fund invests in many bonds, usually hundreds if not thousands. The diversification is excellent. The negative with regard to bond mutual funds is that the bond principal, the money invested, moves directly inverse to the direction of interest rates. So when interest rates are going up the principal is going down, that is bad. However, when interest rates are going down the principal is going up, that is very good.

This also applies to individual bonds. The difference is that bond mutual funds must mark to market daily; the reduction or gain to an investor's account happens immediately. With an individual bond, an investor only realizes the loss or the gain when the bond is sold. If the bond is held until it matures the issuing entity pays back the face value of the bond.

- Bond mutual funds pool assets and must mark to current market prices daily. *The rule of thumb is that for every 1% of interest rate movement, the principal gain or loss will be the inverse direction equal to the duration of the fund.* In other words, if rates go up, the principal will go down and vice versa.

- Duration is an approximate measure of a bond's price sensitivity to changes in interest rates. If a bond has a duration of **6 years**, for example, its price will rise about 6% if its yield drops by a percentage point (100 basis points), and its price will fall by about 6% if its yield rises by that amount. Duration is usually slightly less than the average maturity.

- Bond mutual funds are good investments in a <u>stable or falling interest rate</u> environment.

- To avoid significant principal loss in a rising interest rate environment, select funds with a very short-term duration.

Laddered Maturity Portfolio: Individual bonds and C.D.'s are purchased with the intention of holding them to maturity. Holding the securities to their maturity is a great way to mitigate the effects of changes in interest rates on the principal of the investment. When the security matures, the face value principal is returned to the investor.

Laddering maturities means dividing the portfolio into years, usually not greater than 10 years. Individual bonds and C.D.'s are purchased, e.g. $1/10^{th}$ of the bonds for year one, $1/10^{th}$ for year two, etc. Then each year 1/10 of the portfolio matures and the face value is paid back. New bonds are then purchased at the longest maturity of the ladder. Laddered portfolios may be built with shorter terms, it is important to pick the appropriate timeframe for the investor.

IV
RATING AGENCIES

Rating Agencies for Stocks

Stocks are rated by many analysts and with many different methodologies. Some firm's ratings are just computer model generated with no human analysis.

Two agencies that do a good job, use a consistent methodology and human beings in the analysis process are Standard and Poor's and Morningstar. Both employ a star rating where 1 star is the least rating and 5 stars are the best rating. In practice it is best to compare the ratings of more than one rating company. If the ratings are similar, the better the chance that the analysts may be right.

Morningstar Ratings for Stocks: The Morningstar Rating for stocks identifies stocks trading at a discount or premium to their intrinsic worth or fair value estimate, in Morningstar terminology. *Five-star stocks sell for the biggest risk-adjusted discount to their fair values, whereas 1-star stocks trade at premiums to their intrinsic worth.*

Four key components drive the Morningstar rating: their assessment of the firm's economic moat, estimate of the stock's fair value, uncertainty around that fair value estimate and the current market price. The more uncertain they are about the estimated value of the equity, the greater the discount required relative to the estimate of the value of the firm before a recommendation to purchase the shares is issued. This process ultimately culminates in a star rating.

Morningstar stock 5 star ratings are usually assigned to deep value companies that may have high risk. It is best to be careful with their 5 star ratings relative to stocks.

Morningstar Rating

Price/Fair Value

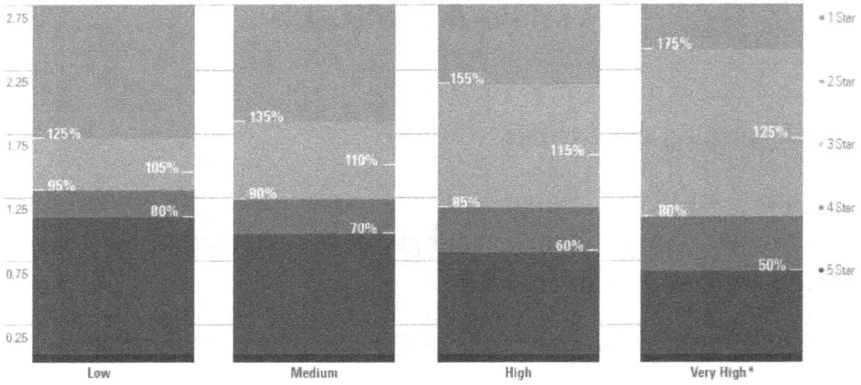

Category	Rating
Low	
Medium	
High	
Very High *	

* Occasionally a stock's uncertainty will be too high for us to estimate, in which case we label it Extreme.

Standard and Poor's Ratings for Stocks:

S&P Capital IQ Equity Research provides unbiased equity analysis and opinion on stocks around the world. S&P Capital IQ incorporates macro and economic analysis with their bottom-up company fundamental and valuation analysis. The STARS Ranking (5 through 1) is the analyst's assessment of potential performance over the next 12-month period.

> ➤ **5-STARS (Strong Buy):** Total return is expected to outperform the total return of the S&P 500 index by a wide margin, with shares rising in absolute price.

> ➤ **4-STARS (Buy):** Total return is expected to outperform the total return of the S&P 500 index, with shares rising in absolute price.

> ➤ **3-STARS (Hold):** Total return is expected to closely approximate that of the S&P 500 index, with shares generally rising in price.

> ➤ **2-STARS (Sell):** Total return is expected to underperform the total return of the S&P 500 index, and share price is not anticipated to show a gain.

> ➢ **1-STARS (Strong Sell):** Total return is expected to underperform the total return of the S&P 500 index, with shares falling in absolute price.

Rating Agencies for Funds

Mutual funds are almost exclusively rated by Morningstar which employs its star rating methodology, but with a completely different assessment than previously discussed for stocks.

Morningstar Ratings for Funds:

The Morningstar Rating™ for funds, often called the "star rating," debuted in 1985 and was quickly embraced by investors and advisors. The Morningstar Rating™ is a quantitative assessment of a fund's past performance—both return and risk—as measured from one to five stars. The rating accounts for all variations in a fund's monthly performance, with more emphasis on downward variations. It rewards consistent performance *(persistency)* and reduces the possibility of strong short-term performance masking the inherent risk of a fund.

Within each Morningstar Category, the top 10% of funds receive 5 stars and the bottom 10% receive 1 star. Funds are rated for up to three time periods: three, five, and 10 years; and these ratings are combined to produce an overall rating. Funds with less than three years of history are not rated.

Ratings are objective, based entirely on a mathematical evaluation of past performance. They're a useful tool for identifying funds worthy of further research, but shouldn't be considered buy or sell signals.

How Does It Work?

The Morningstar Rating™ for funds methodology rates funds based on an enhanced Morningstar Risk-Adjusted Return measure, which also accounts for the effects of all sales charges, loads, or redemption fees. Funds are ranked by their Morningstar Risk-Adjusted Return scores and stars are assigned using the following scale.

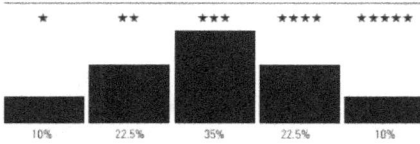

Funds are rated for up to three periods—the trailing three-, five-, and 10-years. For a fund that does not change categories during the evaluation period, the overall rating is calculated using the following weights:

★	★★	★★★	★★★★	★★★★★
10%	22.5%	35%	22.5%	10%

Age of fund	Overall rating
At least three years, but less than five	100% three-year rating
At least five years, but less than 10	60% five-year rating
	40% three-year rating
At least 10 years	50% 10-year rating
	30% five-year rating
	20% three-year rating

Morningstar Analyst Ratings:

Unlike the backward-looking Morningstar Rating™ (often referred to as the "star rating"), the Morningstar Analyst Rating is the summary expression of Morningstar's forward-looking analysis of a fund.

Morningstar analysts assign the ratings on a five-tier scale with
- Three positive ratings of Gold, Silver, and Bronze, a
- Neutral rating, and a
- Negative rating.

The Analyst Rating is based on the analyst's conviction in the fund's ability to outperform its peer group and/or relevant benchmark on a risk-adjusted basis over the long term. If a fund receives a positive rating of Gold, Silver, or Bronze, it means Morningstar analysts think highly of the fund and expect it to outperform over a full market cycle of at least five years.

Rating Agencies for Bonds

The bond credit rating assesses the credit worthiness of a corporation's or government debt issues. The credit rating indicates how likely the company will be to pay interest over the life of the bond; and it also implies indications of the potential marketability of the bonds over their life, as well as the company's ability to return the principal when the bond comes due at maturity.

The credit rating industry is highly concentrated with Moody's Investors Service and Standard & Poor's having roughly 80% market share globally. The "Big Three"— Moody's, S&P and Fitch Ratings — control approximately 95% of the ratings business.

The table below is a synopsis of their ratings. Anything below investment grade is speculative.

Moody's Long-term	S&P Long-term	Fitch Long-term	Rating description	
Aaa	AAA	AAA	Prime	INVESTMENT GRADE
Aa1	AA+	AA+	High grade	INVESTMENT GRADE
Aa2	AA	AA	High grade	INVESTMENT GRADE
Aa3	AA−	AA−	High grade	INVESTMENT GRADE
A1	A+	A+	Upper medium grade	INVESTMENT GRADE
A2	A	A	Upper medium grade	INVESTMENT GRADE
A3	A−	A−	Upper medium grade	INVESTMENT GRADE
Baa1	BBB+	BBB+	Lower medium grade	INVESTMENT GRADE
Baa2	BBB	BBB	Lower medium grade	INVESTMENT GRADE
Baa3	BBB−	BBB−	Lower medium grade	INVESTMENT GRADE
Ba1	BB+	BB+	Non-investment grade	NON INVESTMENT GRADE
Ba2	BB	BB	Speculative	NON INVESTMENT GRADE
Ba3	BB−	BB−		NON INVESTMENT GRADE
B1	B+	B+	Highly speculative	NON INVESTMENT GRADE
B2	B	B	Highly speculative	NON INVESTMENT GRADE
B3	B−	B−	Highly speculative	NON INVESTMENT GRADE
Caa1	CCC+		Substantial risks	NON INVESTMENT GRADE
Caa2	CCC		Extremely speculative	NON INVESTMENT GRADE
Caa3	CCC−	CCC	Default imminent with little	NON INVESTMENT GRADE
Ca	CC	CCC	prospect for recovery	NON INVESTMENT GRADE
Ca	C	CCC	prospect for recovery	NON INVESTMENT GRADE
C	D	DDD	In default	NON INVESTMENT GRADE
/	D	DD, D	In default	NON INVESTMENT GRADE

V
MARKET CYCLES

The Phases of the Business Cycle

This chapter will take a quick look at business cycles and their effect on the global economy.

While no two business cycles are exactly the same, they can be identified as a sequence of four phases that were classified and studied in their most modern sense by American economists Arthur Burns and Wesley Mitchell in their text *Measuring Business Cycles.*

The four primary phases of the business cycle include:

1. **Expansion:** A speedup in the pace of economic activity defined by high growth, low unemployment, and increasing prices. The period marked from trough to peak. This phase also is where the "recovery" occurs.

2. **Peak:** The upper turning point of a business cycle and the point at which expansion turns into contraction.

3. **Contraction:** A slowdown in the pace of economic activity defined by low or stagnant growth, high unemployment, and declining prices. It is the period from peak to trough.

4. **Trough:** The lowest turning point of a business cycle in which a contraction turns into an expansion. This turning point is also called Recovery.

These four phases also make up what is known as the "boom-and-bust" cycles, which are characterized as business cycles in which the periods of expansion are swift and the subsequent contraction is steep and severe.

But What about Recessions?

A recession occurs if a contraction is severe enough. The National Bureau of Economic Research (NBER) identifies a recession as a contraction or significant decline in economic activity "lasting more than a few months, normally visible in real GDP, real income, employment, industrial production."

An investor should know at what point the U.S. and other major global areas such as Europe, China and Japan may be relative to the business cycle. It is a good test along with market valuations to checkup on the business cycle periodically. Then an investor may decide that either a rebalancing of the portfolio would be helpful or a modification of the overall asset allocation, assuming a strategic allocation strategy is being followed.

An example of the global business cycle follows on the next page.

A Business Cycle pictorial view is published by Fidelity on a regular basis. They plot major countries along the curve showing where they are relative to the macro cycle. Below is a sample of that snapshot from the fall of 2015.

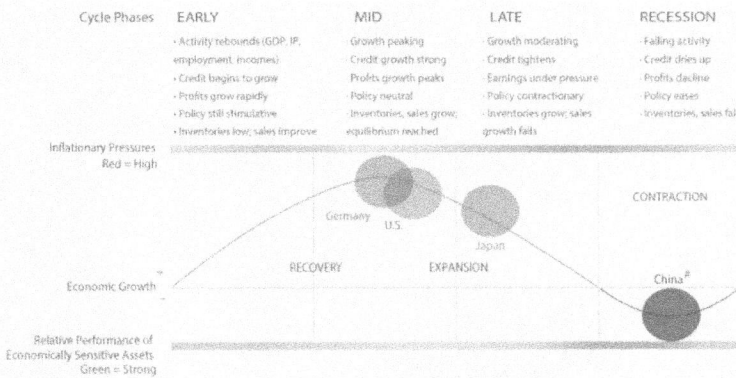

Note: The diagram above is a hypothetical illustration of the business cycle. There is not always a chronological, linear progression among the phases of the business cycle, and there have been cycles when the economy has skipped a phase or retraced an earlier one. #A growth recession is a significant decline in activity relative to a country's long-term economic potential. We have adopted the "growth cycle" definition for most developing economies, such as China, because they tend to exhibit strong trend performance driven by rapid factor accumulation and increases in productivity, and the deviation from the trend tends to matter the most for asset returns. We use the classic definition of recession, involving an outright contraction in economic activity, for developed economies. Please see endnotes for a complete discussion. Source: Fidelity Investments (AART).

Continuing the process of building an investment plan, the next step is to determine an appropriate Asset Allocation to the major asset classes.

VI
ASSET ALLOCATION

Asset Allocation involves dividing an investment portfolio among different asset categories, such as stocks, bonds, and cash.

The process of determining which mix of assets to hold in a portfolio is a very personal one. The asset allocation that works best for an investor at any given point in life will depend largely on the investor's time horizon and ability to tolerate risk.

➢ **Time Horizon** - Time horizon is the expected number of months, years, or decades an investor will be investing to achieve a particular financial goal. An investor with a longer time horizon may feel more comfortable taking on a riskier, or more volatile, investment because he or she can wait out slow economic cycles and the inevitable ups and downs of our markets. By contrast, an investor saving for a short-term goal would likely take on less risk because he or she has a shorter time horizon.

➢ **Risk Tolerance** - Risk tolerance is an investor's ability and willingness to lose some or all of an original investment in exchange for greater potential returns. An aggressive investor, or one with a high-risk tolerance, is more likely to risk losing money in order to get better results. A conservative investor, or one with a low-risk tolerance, tends to favor investments that will preserve his or her original investment.

When it comes to investing, risk and reward are inextricably entwined. The reward for taking on risk is the potential for a greater investment return. For example, if the time horizon for financial goals is longer term, investing in asset categories with greater risk (e.g. stocks) is likely to make more money compared to investments with low risk (e.g. cash equivalents). Investing solely in cash investments may be appropriate for short-term financial goals or for an investor with a very low risk tolerance.

Although an investor's exact asset allocation should depend on the goals for the money, some rules of thumb exist to guide decisions. The most important asset allocation decision is the split or ratio between risky and non-risky assets, often referred to as the stock to bond split or ratio.

Below are comments on the subject from two well-known investors. Note that they both clearly have a place for bonds in every allocation scenario.

John Bogle, the founder of The Vanguard Group, writes:

"..., I recommended -- as a crude starting point -- that an investor's bond position should be equal to his or her age. An investor age 65, then, would consider the propriety of a 65/35 bond/stock allocation. Clearly, such a rule must be adjusted to reflect an investor's objectives, risk tolerance, and overall financial position. (For example, pension and Social Security payments would be considered bond like investments.) But the point is that as we age, we usually have (1) more wealth to protect, (2) less time to recoup severe losses, (3) greater need for income, and (4) perhaps an increased nervousness as markets jump around. All four of these factors suggest more bonds as we age."

(John Bogle, Bogleheads.com; 2010 edition of Common Sense on Mutual Funds, pp.87-88).

Benjamin Graham's timeless advice:

"We have suggested as a fundamental guiding rule that the investor should never have less than 25% or more than 75% of his funds in common stocks, with a consequence inverse range of 75% to 25% in bonds. There is an implication here that the standard division should be an equal one, or 50-50, between the two major investment mediums."

(Benjamin Graham, The Intelligent Investor).

Let's take a closer look at the major asset classes utilized in investing a portfolio. The level of risk one will experience is different for each choice.

➢ **Stocks** - Stocks have historically had the greatest risk and highest returns among the three major asset categories. As an asset category, stocks are a portfolio's biggest return class, offering the greatest potential for growth. Stocks may achieve big returns but also may produce big losses. The volatility of stocks makes them a very risky investment in the short term. Within this asset class there are four major sub-categories:

- U.S. Stocks
- Non-U.S. Stocks
- Real Estate Securities
- Commodity-Linked Securities

➢ **Bonds** - Bonds are generally less volatile than stocks but offer more modest returns. As a result, an investor approaching a financial goal might increase the allocation to this asset class, because the reduced risk of holding more bonds would be attractive to the investor despite their lower potential for growth. Make note that Bonds carry increased principal risk when interest rates are rising; more on this subject later.

➢ **Cash** - Cash and cash equivalents - such as savings deposits, certificates of deposit, treasury bills, money market deposit accounts, and money market funds - are the safest investments, but offer the lowest return of the three major asset categories. The chances of losing money on an investment in this asset category are generally extremely low. The major concern for investors investing in cash equivalents is inflation risk. This is the risk that inflation will outpace and erode investment returns over time.

For the purpose of the Asset Allocation discussion, the above asset classes will be divided into two groups:

- *Risk Assets: Stocks*
- *Fixed Income: Bonds and Cash.*

Risk assets are the investments that will be subjected to the most risk, while the fixed income segment will be the more stable, conservative portion of the portfolio.

The charts and tables below provide a look at single asset class returns over long periods of time. The risk of loss and the difference in returns is very apparent.

100% bonds

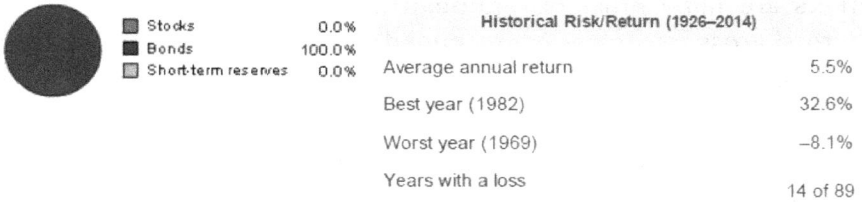

			Historical Risk/Return (1926–2014)	
Stocks	0.0%			
Bonds	100.0%			
Short-term reserves	0.0%	Average annual return	5.5%
		Best year (1982)	32.6%
		Worst year (1969)	−8.1%
		Years with a loss	14 of 89

100% stocks

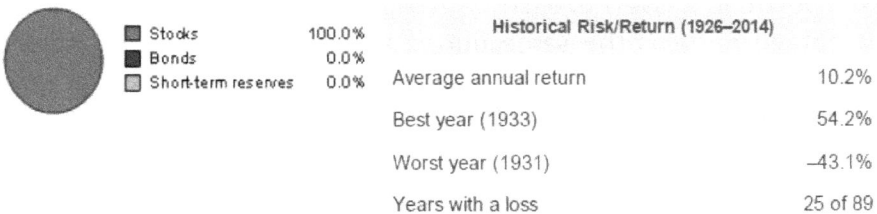

			Historical Risk/Return (1926–2014)	
Stocks	100.0%			
Bonds	0.0%			
Short-term reserves	0.0%	Average annual return	10.2%
		Best year (1933)	54.2%
		Worst year (1931)	−43.1%
		Years with a loss	25 of 89

By including multiple asset categories with investment returns that move up and down under different market conditions within a portfolio, an investor can help protect against significant losses. Historically, the returns of the three major asset categories have not moved up and down at the same time. Market conditions that cause one asset category to do well often cause another asset category to have average or poor returns. Recent market experience during downturns, however, has not been as encouraging.

By investing in more than one asset category, the objective is that an investor's portfolio will have a smoother ride. We will delve more deeply into this subject in the next chapter.

Two strategies are discussed below that are common management strategies. The investment strategies employed are long term investment strategies where investments are normally held for many years and is not intended to market time and do not chase speculative investments. The investment approach is rooted in the belief that markets are fairly efficient, although not always rational, and that investors' gross returns are determined principally by asset allocation decisions.

Strategies:

Fixed Allocation: A **fixed portfolio allocation** assigns a percentage of the portfolio's assets to each asset class: stocks, bonds and cash. This percentage remains the same during all market conditions and the investment timeframe. The strategy rebalances to the set allocation percentage at least once a year.

Strategic Allocation: A **strategic portfolio allocation** assigns a *range of percentages* to the portfolio's assets for each asset class: stocks, bonds and cash. The actual percentage allocation assigned is determined based on the business cycle and overall market valuation. When the market is overvalued the lower percentage within the range is assigned; when the market is undervalued the higher percentage within the range is assigned. The strategy rebalances to the set allocation percentage at least once a year. The target allocations are determined at the time of the rebalancing and may or may not be changed. The objective of this strategy is to sell a portion of the risk assets at or near market "highs" and to buy more risk assets at or near market "lows".

Either strategy will work fine. It is a personal preference whether to keep it simple and employ a "fixed allocation", or pay more attention to market cycles and utilize a "strategic allocation".

Essentially what asset allocation is doing is dividing the money up into separate baskets to invest in different asset classes; some asset classes are riskier than others. The highest level of asset allocation is the percentage allocated between stocks and fixed income (including bonds, C.D.'s and cash). Then these major asset classes must be diversified into many investments and sub-classes to mitigate risk. Diversification is a subject that will be covered in the next chapter.

Let's apply the information that has been gathered so far: risk tolerance, time horizon, etc.; and determine an allocation for stocks or risk assets. On the next page, guidelines are provided based on several investment timeframes and risk tolerance categories.

The following table is a representative guideline for determining an appropriate portfolio allocation to *risk assets only*, i.e. stocks.

Risk Asset Allocations Guidelines	Strategic Allocation		Fixed Allocation Strategy	Bond Quality
	Over-Valued Market	*Under-Valued Market*		
General Timeframe: 10 Years or More				
Very Conservative	0%	10%	5%	US Gov.
Conservative	10%	30%	20%	AA
Moderately Conservative	25%	45%	35%	A
Moderate	40%	60%	50%	A-
Moderate Growth	50%	70%	60%	BBB+
Moderately Aggressive	60%	80%	70%	BBB
Aggressive	75%	95%	85%	BBB
	Over-Valued Market	*Under-Valued Market*	Fixed Allocation Strategy	Bond Quality
Nearing Retirement: 5 Years or <				
Very Conservative	0%	5%	0%	US Gov.
Conservative	5%	25%	15%	AA
Moderately Conservative	15%	35%	25%	A
Moderate	30%	50%	40%	A-
Moderate Growth	40%	60%	50%	BBB+
Moderately Aggressive	50%	70%	60%	BBB
Aggressive	60%	80%	70%	BBB
	Over-Valued Market	*Under-Valued Market*	Fixed Allocation Strategy	Bond Quality
Retired:				
Very Conservative & Ret. Elderly	0%	5%	0%	US Gov.
Conservative	0%	10%	5%	AA
Moderately Conservative	5%	25%	15%	A
Moderate	20%	40%	30%	A-
Moderate Growth	30%	50%	40%	BBB+
Moderately Aggressive	40%	60%	50%	BBB
Aggressive	50%	70%	60%	BBB

The General Timeframe "Fixed Allocation" was developed by averaging recommended allocation by Charles Schwab, Fidelity and Vanguard. The nearing retirement and retired sections are more conservative extrapolations. Strategic allocation ranges utilize the respective "fixed allocation" as a mid-point of the ranges.

The table above has three sections, each for a different investment timeframe.

- 10 years or more
- 5 years or less
- Retired (this section would also apply to any situation where the use of the money has already arrived)

Within each section are several risk tolerance categories and the associated asset allocation percentages for stocks and risk assets for that particular risk tolerance.

- ➢ For the *Strategic Allocation strategy*, the allocation ranges for this strategy are the first two columns.

- ➢ For the *Fixed Allocation* strategy, the percentage allocation to risk assets are in the column highlighted.

- ➢ The last column is the guideline for Bond quality minimum rating indicated by Standard & Poor's ratings; Moody's has a similar and corresponding rating that is also widely used.

As mentioned, Portfolio Allocations between risk assets (or stocks) and fixed income (bonds and cash) are an individual decision based on individual circumstances; considering the investor's objectives, risk tolerance, and overall financial position.

All age-based guidelines are predicated on the assumption that an individual's circumstances mirror the general populations. Individuals with different retirement ages (earlier or later), asset levels, or needs for the money would be well-advised to consider what circumstances make their situation different and adjust their asset allocation accordingly.

Investors choosing to use less conservative guidelines, i.e. more aggressive, should understand why they feel the need, ability, and willingness to take on the greater inherent risk.

Select the worksheet below that corresponds to the chosen investment strategy and fill in the selected allocations for Risk Assets.

Then to derive the fixed income allocation, subtract this allocation from 100% and fill the results in under Fixed Income; do this calculation for each column. The result is your chosen allocation to risk assets and fixed income.

FIXED ALLOCATION STRATEGY:	
	FIXED %
Risk Assets - Stocks	
Fixed Income	

STRATEGIC ALLOCATION STRATEGY:			
	Over-Valued %	Under-Valued %	Mid-Point %
Risk Assets - Stocks			
Fixed Income			

VII
DIVERSIFICATION

It is true that the greater the risk, the greater the potential rewards in investing, but taking on unnecessary risk is often avoidable. Investors will best protect themselves against risk by spreading their money among various investments, hoping that if one investment loses money, the other investments will more than make up for those losses. This strategy, called "diversification," can be neatly summed up as, "Don't put all your eggs in one basket."

Why diversify?

1 Diversification can help manage risk.

2 You may avoid costly mistakes by adopting a risk level you can live with.

3 Rebalancing is a key to maintaining risk levels over time.

The goal of diversification is not to boost performance—it won't ensure gains or guarantee against losses. But once an investor chooses to target a level of risk based on appropriate goals, time horizon, and tolerance for volatility; diversification may provide the potential to improve returns for a given level of risk. To say it differently, diversification attempts to eliminate or reduce the likelihood that one investment or type of investment will rule the portfolio either positively or negatively.

To build a diversified portfolio, look for assets—stocks, bonds, cash, or others—whose returns haven't historically moved in the same direction, and ideally, assets whose returns typically move in opposite directions. This way, even if a portion of the portfolio is declining, the rest of the portfolio, hopefully, is growing. A well-diversified portfolio will not only be comprised of the different asset classes and sub classes, but will comprise many investments within each class.

Within the individual *stock holdings*, beware of overconcentration in a single stock. For example, one stock should not make up more than 5% of the portfolio. It's smart to diversify across stocks by market capitalization (small, mid, and large caps), sectors, and geography. Not all caps, sectors, and regions have prospered at the same time, or to the same degree, so the portfolio risk may be reduced by spreading the assets across different parts of the stock market. In addition the style of the stock, such as growth and value, may be considered; these tend to perform at different rates depending on the point in the business cycle.

Similarly, when it comes to an investor's *bond investments*, consider varying maturities, credit qualities and durations, which measure sensitivity to interest-rate changes.

The following charts and tables provide some historic data. Consider the performance of three hypothetical portfolios:

1. All-cash portfolio;
2. A diversified portfolio of 70% stocks, 25% bonds, and 5% short-term investments;
3. 100% stock portfolio.

Diversification helped limit losses and capture gains during the 2008 financial crisis

	Jan. 2008 through the market bottom, Feb. 2009	Five years from the bottom: Mar. 2009–Feb. 2014	2008 to five years from bottom: Jan. 2008–Feb. 2014
All-cash portfolio	1.6%	0.3%	2.0%
Diversified portfolio	−35.0%	99.7%	29.9%
All-stock portfolio	−49.7%	162.3%	31.8%

Source: Strategic Advisers, Inc. Chart is for illustrative purposes only and is not indicative of any investment. Past performance is no guarantee of future results.

The sample asset mixes below combine various amounts of stock, bond, and short-term investments to illustrate different levels of risk and return potential (1926 – 2014).

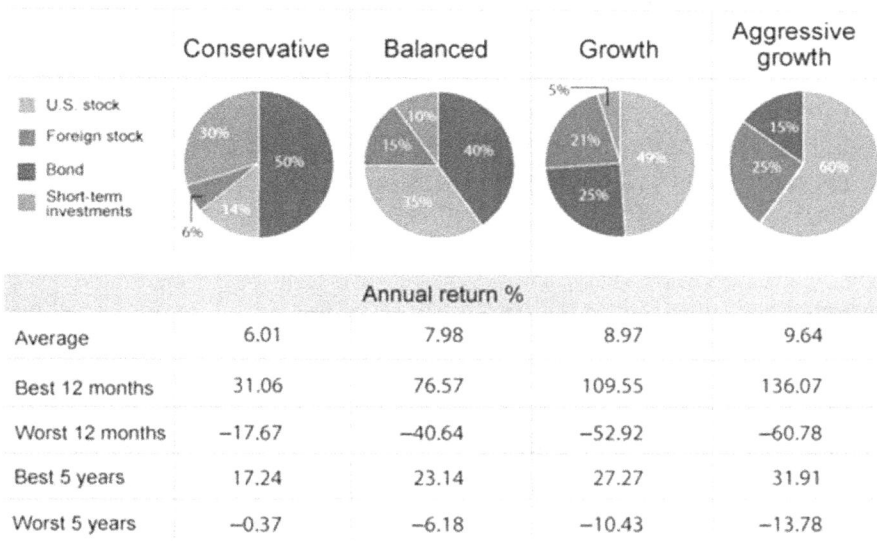

	Conservative	Balanced	Growth	Aggressive growth
Annual return %				
Average	6.01	7.98	8.97	9.64
Best 12 months	31.06	76.57	109.55	136.07
Worst 12 months	−17.67	−40.64	−52.92	−60.78
Best 5 years	17.24	23.14	27.27	31.91
Worst 5 years	−0.37	−6.18	−10.43	−13.78

Data Source: Ibbotson Associates, 2015 (1926–2014). **Past performance is no guarantee of future results.** Returns include the reinvestment of dividends and other earnings. This chart is for illustrative purposes only and does not represent actual or implied performance of any investment option.

The above charts drive home the point that the more risky the investments, the greater the chance for gains; but also the greater the chance for losses. Over long periods of time higher risk usually pays off. But, the danger is over concentration to one investment or asset class.

The following discussion will explain how the different investment choices and sub-categories may help to diversify a portfolio.

U.S. Stocks

U.S. Stocks are shares of companies that are domiciled in the U.S. There are roughly 6,000 companies on the NYSE and NASDAQ combined. These companies may be separated into asset class categories by size of the company and by the business sector they belong to.

By Size of company:

- **Large-cap stocks:** A term used by the investment community to refer to companies with a market capitalization value of more than $10 billion. Large-cap is an abbreviation of the term "large market capitalization". Market capitalization is calculated by multiplying the number of a company's shares outstanding by its stock price per share.

- **Mid-cap stocks:** A company with a market capitalization between $2 and $10 billion.

- **Small-cap stocks:** Refers to stocks with a relatively small market capitalization. The definition of small cap can vary among brokerages, but generally it is a company with a market capitalization of between $300 million and $2 billion.

By Business Sector: Global Industry Classification Standard (GICS) developed by MSCI and Standard & Poor's.

- Consumer Discretionary
- Consumer Staples
- Energy
- Financials
- Healthcare
- Industrials
- Information Technology
- Materials
- Telecommunication Services
- Utilities

Non-U.S. Stocks

Non-U.S. equities currently account for close to 55% of global market capitalization, thus representing a significant opportunity for U.S. investors. In addition, the portfolio of an investor who combined non-U.S. equities with U.S. equities over the past several decades would have experienced lower average volatility—despite similar realized returns and volatilities in each region.

- Developed markets such as Europe, Australia and Japan have lower risk than emerging economies
- The recent correlation of foreign markets to the U.S. has been increasing, making this asset sub-class somewhat less opportunistic than in the past; it remains to be seen whether this pattern will continue.
- Currency fluctuations have periodically added or subtracted from returns. When the U.S. dollar is very strong it creates headwinds for foreign investments.

Real Estate Securities

Real estate is undoubtedly a significant element of asset allocation, and should form a component of any personal investment portfolio.

- If one owns the home they live in, they are already invested in real estate; the percentage this amounts to relative to the overall portfolio may be enough for this category. It is important to quantify this amount.
- REITS or Real Estate Investment Trusts have a low-to-moderate correlation with other sectors of the stock market, as well as bonds and other assets. They are easy to invest in and usually provide regular income through dividends.
- Interest rate increases by the Federal Reserve tend to impact the price of REITS securities in a negative manner; especially in the beginning of the cycle.

Commodity-Linked Securities

Commodities are raw materials that are sold in bulk, such as oil, wheat, silver, gold, pork bellies, oranges and cocoa. They are generally raw materials that are eventually used to produce other goods such as oil for gasoline, cocoa for chocolate, wheat for bread, etc. As such, they give an investor the opportunity to invest in the materials that a country (or corporation) produces as well as those that it consumes.

- A *commodity-linked security* refers to a security whose return is dependent to a certain extent on the price level of a commodity, such as crude oil, gold, or silver, at maturity. For example, the principal of a commodity-linked bond is indexed to movements of a commodity index such as precious metal or oil.
- Commodities can be very volatile and may have the perception of higher risk.
- One needs to understand the basic fundamentals for the commodity that he or she may invest in.
- This sub-class is one that requires special knowledge and careful analysis

At the same time that the stock market is experiencing ups and downs, the bond market is fluctuating as well. That's why asset allocation, or including different types of investments in a portfolio, is such an important strategy. In many cases, the bond market is up when the stock market is down and vice versa. An investor's goal is to be invested in several categories of investments at the same time, so that some of the money will be in the category that's doing well at any given time.

Bonds:

To better understand bonds and bond funds, let's start with some basic concepts.

A bond is a loan that an investor makes to a corporation, government, federal agency or other organization. Consequently, bonds are sometimes referred to as debt securities. The issuer of the bond (the borrower) enters into a legal agreement to pay the investor (the bondholder) interest, this is also called the "coupon". The bond issuer also agrees to repay the investor the original sum loaned at the bond's maturity date, though certain conditions, such as a bond being called, may cause repayment to be made earlier.

The vast majority of bonds have a set maturity date—a specific date when the bond must be paid back at its face value, called par value. Bonds are called fixed-income securities because many pay interest based on a regular, predetermined interest rate—also called a coupon rate—that is set when the bond is issued. Similarly, the term "bond market" is often used interchangeably with "fixed income market."

Bond Maturity: A bond's **term**, or years to maturity, is usually set when it is issued. The majority of bond maturities range from one to 30 years. Bonds are often referred to as being short-, medium- or long-term.

- Generally, a bond that matures in one to three years is referred to as a *short-term bond.*
- *Medium- or intermediate-term bonds* are generally those that mature in four to 10 years, and
- *Long-term bonds* are those with maturities greater than 10 years.

The borrower fulfills its debt obligation typically when the bond reaches its maturity date, and the final interest payment and the original sum loaned (the principal) are paid to the bondholder.

Understanding Interest-Rate Risk:

Bonds tend to rise in value when interest rates fall, and they fall in value when interest rates rise. Usually, the longer the maturity of the bond, the greater the price volatility will be. This is known as interest rate risk. If an investor holds a bond until maturity, these price fluctuations are of little concern; because at maturity, the investor will receive the par, or face value of the bond.

This inverse relationship between bond prices and interest rates is essentially straightforward as explained below:

- When interest rates rise, new issues come to market with higher yields than older securities, making those older ones worth less. Hence, their prices go down.
- When interest rates decline, new bond issues come to market with lower yields than older securities, making those older, higher-yielding ones worth more. Hence, their prices go up.

As a result, if a bond must be sold before maturity, it may be worth more or less than originally paid for it, depending on the change in interest rates since the purchase.

Various economic forces affect the level and direction of interest rates in the economy. Interest rates typically climb when the economy is growing, and fall during economic downturns. Similarly, rising inflation leads to rising interest rates, although at some point, higher rates themselves become contributors to higher inflation; and moderating inflation leads to lower interest rates. Inflation is one of the most influential forces on interest rates.

The "rule of thumb" is that for every 1% of interest rate movement, the principal gain or loss will be the inverse direction equal to the duration of the fund.

As a reminder, *duration* is an approximate measure of a bond's price sensitivity to changes in interest rates. If a bond has a duration of 6 years, for example, its price will rise about 6% if its yield drops by a percentage point (100 basis points), and its price will fall by about 6% if its yield rises by that amount. Duration is usually slightly less than the average maturity.

Selecting a mix of different issuers and industries would diversify a bond portfolio. The following classes of bonds are examples:

▪ U.S. Government Obligations: Treasury bills, notes and bonds, U.S. Agency bonds and FDIC Insured C.D's would be selected depending on which ones provide the best risk/return at the time they are being acquired.

▪ Corporate Bonds: A mix of investment grade ratings would be selected as long as the lower end of the investment ratings does not dominate the allocation.

▪ Municipal Bonds: For favorable tax purposes in a taxable account, selecting bonds from an investor's tax state would be preferred. However, often because of limited availability of sufficient bonds other states may need to be utilized. It is best to select General Obligation bonds that are rated AA or better by Standard & Poor's or the Moody's equivalent.

▪ Treasury Inflation Protected Securities (TIPS) may be included as a component of the portfolio for their inflation protection attributes.

Cash
The last class is cash. It is the safest of all investments, but generally returns the least in the way of growth or interest income. Bank accounts, C.D. and money market accounts make up the bulk of this category. Bank accounts and C.D.'s are generally insured by the FDIC up to $250,000 per depositor at any given financial institution.

The following charts depict the correlation of various asset classes. The less correlated the better the diversification potential and mitigation of risk to one asset class.

MONTHLY CORRELATIONS BETWEEN MARKET SEGMENTS AND U.S. STOCKS AND BONDS: 1988-2011

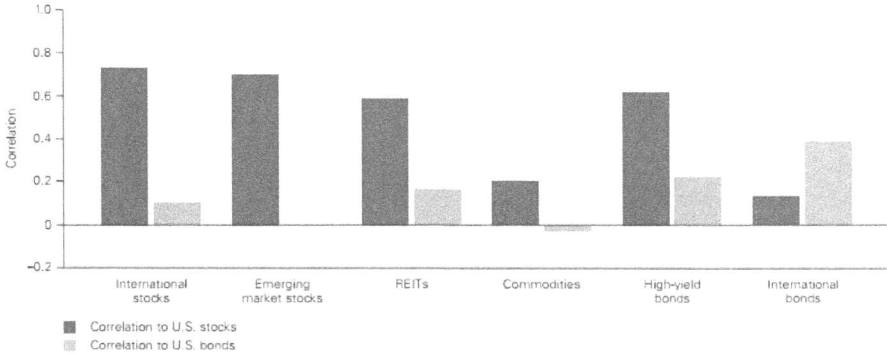

Correlation to U.S. stocks
Correlation to U.S. bonds

Notes: U.S. stocks are represented by the Dow Jones U.S. Total Stock Market Index from 1988 through April 22, 2005, and the MSCI US Broad Market Index thereafter; U.S. bonds are represented by the Barclays Capital U.S. Aggregate Bond Index; international stocks are represented by the MSCI EAFE Index; emerging market stocks are represented by the MSCI Emerging Markets Index; REITs are represented by the FTSE NAREIT Index; commodities are represented by the S&P GSCI Total Return Index from 1988 through 1990 and the Dow Jones UBS Commodities Index thereafter; high-yield bonds are represented by the Barclays Capital High Yield Bond Index, and international bonds are represented by the Citigroup World Global Bond Index ex U.S. from 1988 through 1989 and the Barclays Capital Global Aggregate ex U.S. Bond Index thereafter.

Sources: Vanguard calculations, using data provided by Thomson Reuters Datastream.

MONTHLY CORRELATIONS BETWEEN MARKET SEGMENTS AND U.S. STOCKS AND BONDS: OCTOBER 2007 – FEBRUARY 2009

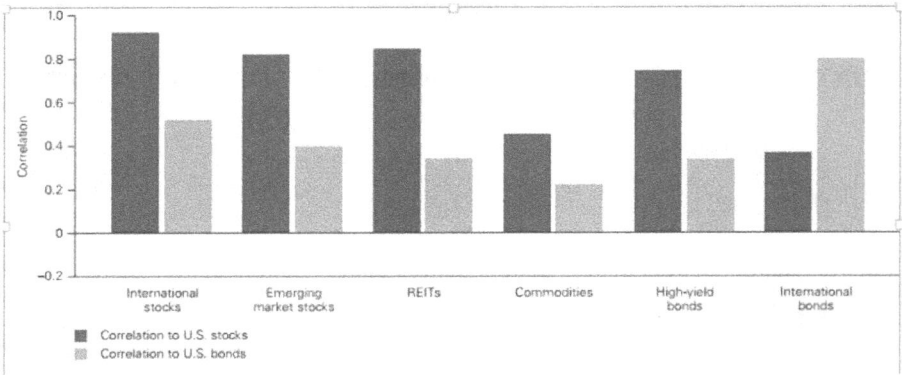

Notes: A similar spike in correlations was observed in 1998, a period characterized by the Asian Contagion, the Russian debt default, and the collapse of Long-Term Capital Management.
Sources: Vanguard calculations, using data provided by Thomson Reuters Datastream.

When thinking about portfolio diversification, investors instinctively focus on correlation. Yet, as the above tables have shown, combining assets with low historical correlation does not eliminate risk, or the adverse co-movement in times of crisis. Still, discussions of the benefits of diversification often overlook the fact that while assets with low historical correlation can move in the same direction, they rarely, if ever, move in the same direction with the same magnitude.

Looking at the chart from October 2007 through February 2009, a period representing the worst of the recent bear market; the correlation of most risk assets to U.S. Stocks was close to 1.0, i.e. moving in unison in the same direction. There was some relief with commodities and international bonds. This period was abnormal, but demonstrates the high risk at times of crisis. Essentially during this period there was nowhere to hide, except in cash.

Let's apply the principles of diversification to the major asset classes and sub-classes. The resulting allocations are then based on their relative risk, where the more risky classes are assigned a lesser allocation.

The tables below are representative examples of these allocations. *To simplify the discussion, we will view each section, Stock or Fixed Income, separately totaling 100% for that section.*

Stock Asset Class Category	Range of Allocation
1. Large Capitalization U.S. Stocks	30-60%
2. Mid-Capitalization U S. Stocks	10-20%
3. Small Capitalization U S. Stocks	5-10%
4. International (non-U.S.) Company Stocks	10-25%
5. Emerging Market Stocks	0-5%
6. Individual Sector over-weighting	0-10%

Fixed Income Asset Class Category	Range of Allocation
1. U.S. Treasury/Agency bills, notes, bonds & C.D.'s	20-80%
2. U.S. Corporate Bonds Investment Grade	20-50%
3. Treasury Inflation Protected Securities	0-20%
4. Municipal Bonds	0-35%
5. Closed-end Bond Funds	0-10%
6. Cash, Money Market, T-bills	5-25%

The table below is a reasonable representation of an entire portfolio presented by individual investor risk tolerance categories. The time frame for the financial goals or the need for the money is considered to be longer term in this example.

Strategy	Asset allocation:			
	Domestic stock	Foreign stock	Bonds	Short-term
Conservative	14%	6	50%	30%
Moderate with income	21%	9%	50%	20%
Moderate	28%	12%	45%	15%
Balanced	35%	15%	40%	10
Growth with income	42%	18%	35%	5
Growth	49%	21%	25%	5
Aggressive growth	60%		25%	15%
All stock	70%		30%	

Source: Fidelity Investments, "Sample Allocations".

It is important to reiterate at this point that assessing one's proper risk tolerance is critical to long term investing success. From this assessment an appropriate overall allocation ratio to risk assets and fixed income may be determined and written into an investment policy statement. If the investor then follows this blueprint for the investment portfolio makeup, it will be easier to sleep at night and maintain proper investing discipline.

Applying the theoretical principles of asset allocation and diversification, in the next chapter we will develop Model Portfolios of actual ETFs and Mutual Funds.

VIII
MODEL PORTFOLIOS

Selecting the right investments is important. In the prior chapters we have discussed asset allocation, diversification and rating agencies for stocks. All of these activities come into play when building a portfolio.

The basic allocation to risk assets and fixed income was discussed in the chapter on Asset Allocation. Examples of a good mix of sub-categories was provided in the chapter on Diversification. The Rating Agency chapter discussed the ratings from Morningstar and Standard & Poor's for stocks and mutual funds. *Ideally selecting investments rated with the four or five star ratings is preferred*, however, sometimes that is not always possible and a deeper look into the investments is necessary to complete the analysis for their selection.

When building a portfolio, the beauty of mutual funds or ETFs (Exchange Traded Funds) is one fund generally will be made up of hundreds of securities; whereas with individual stocks a minimum of 25 to 50 different stocks is necessary in different industries to provide reasonable diversification.

Before discussing model portfolio selection, let's review the criteria for selecting a mutual fund:

✓ No sales charges, i.e. "No Load" funds

✓ A low expense ratio (below 1.00%)

✓ Morningstar Ratings of 4 or 5 star is preferred, also a

✓ Morningstar analysts ranking of Bronze, Silver or Gold is preferred

There are terrific fund families that meet the above criteria; several are listed below. The first three families have a robust mix of funds that meet this criteria to choose from; the remaining fund families either specialize in certain sectors or have fewer no-load funds in their stable.

- ➢ Fidelity
- ➢ Vanguard
- ➢ T. Rowe Price
- American Century
- Oakmark
- Blackrock
- PIMCO

Two model portfolios are presented herein as an examples of how to build a diversified portfolio with less than ten funds. These portfolios are not intended to be a short-cut to investing. The performance, managers running the funds, or other characteristics may change from time to time. *It is important to do your own research when selecting funds for a portfolio, it's called due diligence.*

Model Portfolio 1 is comprised of all ETFs and Model Portfolio 2 is all no-load mutual funds. Both portfolios achieve similar diversification, expected performance and low expense ratios. The Mutual Fund portfolio (Portfolio 2) contains some managed and index tracking funds.

Each section of the portfolios, i.e. Equity Securities (Stocks) and Fixed Income, is presented as a separate 100% allocation. Presented this way allows the allocation of funds consistently regardless of what the stock to bond ratio may be.

For example, if money was to be allocated 60% to Stocks and 40% to Fixed Income, then

- For the stock section take 60% of the money and divide it up as shown in the model portfolio section headed "EQUITY SECURITIES (STOCKS)"; then
- For the fixed income allocation apply 40% of the money to the "Fixed Income" funds.

MODEL PORTFOLIO 1: EXCHANGE TRADED FUNDS - ETFs

EQUITY SECURITIES (STOCKS):	Ticker	Exp. Ratio	Div. Rate	STYLE	Target Alloc.	MSTAR
iShares S&P 500	IVV	0.07%	2.25%	L BLEND	50%	4 STAR
iShares S&P Midcap 400	IJH	0.12%	1.50%	MID	15%	4 STAR
iShares S&P Small cap 600	IJR	0.12%	1.50%	SMALL	10%	5 STAR
iShares MSCI EAFE Min. Volatility	EFAV	0.20%	2.50%	INTL	20%	5 STAR
iShares MSCI Emerging Mkt. Min. Vol.	EEMV	0.25%	2.50%	Emerge	5%	4 STAR
TOTAL EQUITY SECURITIES . . .					100%	

FIXED INCOME:	Ticker	Exp. Ratio	Div. Rate	STYLE	Target Alloc.	MSTAR
Cash - Money Market			0.10%		20%	
Vanguard Short-Term Corp	VCSH	0.10%	1.60%	Short-term	20%	5 STAR
iShares Core US Aggregate Bond	AGG	0.08%	2.30%	Intermediate	60%	3 STAR
TOTAL FIXED INCOME					100%	

MODEL PORTFOLIO 2: MUTUAL FUNDS

EQUITY SECURITIES (STOCKS):	Ticker	Exp. Ratio	Div. Rate	STYLE	Target Alloc.	MSTAR
Fidelity Spartan 500 Index	FUSEX	0.09%	2.25%	L BLEND	25%	4 STAR
Vanguard Dividend Growth	VDIGX	0.32%	1.91%	L BLEND	25%	5 STAR
Vanguard Midcap Index I	VMCIX	0.08%	1.59%	MID BL	15%	4 STAR
Vanguard Small-cap Index I Inv	NAESX	0.23%	1.46%	SMALL	10%	4 STAR
Fidelity International Discovery	FIGRX	0.98%	1.11%	INTL	20%	4 STAR
Oppenheimer Developing Mkts I	ODVIX	0.86%	1.05%	Emerge	5%	4 STAR
TOTAL EQUITY SECURITIES . . .					**100%**	

FIXED INCOME:	Ticker	Exp. Ratio	Div. Rate	STYLE	Target Alloc.	MSTAR
Cash - Money Market			0.10%		20%	
Vanguard Short-Term Bond	VBISX	0.20%	1.25%	Short-term	20%	4 STAR
Fidelity Spartan US Bond Idx	FBIDX	0.22%	2.37%	Intermediate	30%	3 STAR
Fidelity Total Bond	FTBFX	0.45%	3.10%	Intermediate	30%	4 STAR
TOTAL FIXED INCOME. . . .					**100%**	

A note about the fixed income – bond – selections above: both model portfolios are presenting a mix of funds for a normal investing environment and interest rate environment.

If the investing environment is such that rates are either rising or expected to rise and the purchase of individual bonds or C.D.'s is not feasible; then as an alternative to holding individual bonds to mitigate this risk, short duration bond funds may be utilized.

Remember, in a rising interest rate environment principal loss is a significant risk. The "rule of thumb" is that for every 1% of interest rate movement, the principal gain or loss will be the inverse direction equal to the duration of the fund.

Short duration funds will have less volatility in a rising interest rate environment than intermediate or long-term bond funds since their timeframe to maturity is short term. *However, they do not completely eliminate interest rate risk or the potential loss of principal.*

An example of these short duration funds is provided below. Again, it is important to do your own due diligence when selecting funds for a portfolio.

Short-term Duration Bond Funds as Alternative:					
	Ticker	Exp. Ratio	Div. Rate	Duration	MSTAR
PIMCO Enhanced Short Maturity	MINT	0.35%	0.86%	0.32	3 STAR
Fidelity Short-term Bond Fund	FSHBX	0.45%	1.00%	1.65	3 STAR
iShares 1-3 Year Credit Bond	CSJ	0.20%	1.19%	1.90	3 STAR
SPDR Barclays Short-term Corp	SCPB	0.10%	1.44%	2.00	4 STAR
Vanguard Short-term Corp	VCSH	0.10%	2.00%	2.74	5 STAR
Vanguard Short-term Bond Index Adm.	VBIRX	0.10%	1.30%	2.70	4 STAR

Note:

Morningstar ratings (MSTAR) are the ratings in effect at the time of this writing approximately February, 2016.

IX
REBALANCING

Diversification is not a one-time task.

Once a target allocation mix is developed, it needs to be kept on track with periodic checkups and rebalancing back to the target allocations. If rebalancing is not performed, a good run in stocks could leave a portfolio with a risk level that is inconsistent with the investor's goals and strategy.

What if a portfolio is not rebalanced? Let's look at a hypothetical portfolio over an historical 20-year period to illustrate how changing markets, such as a prior year's large rise in the S&P 500, can have an impact on an investment mix; and in turn, on the amount of risk in a portfolio.

Consider a hypothetical growth portfolio in April 1995, with:

- 70% in stocks (49% U.S. and 21% foreign),
- 25% bonds, and
- 5% short-term investments.

Two decades later at the end of March 2015, the investment mix has changed dramatically to more than: (see the chart below)

- 80% in stocks (67% U.S. and 14% foreign),
- 17% in bonds, and
- 2% short term.

How an investment mix can change over time

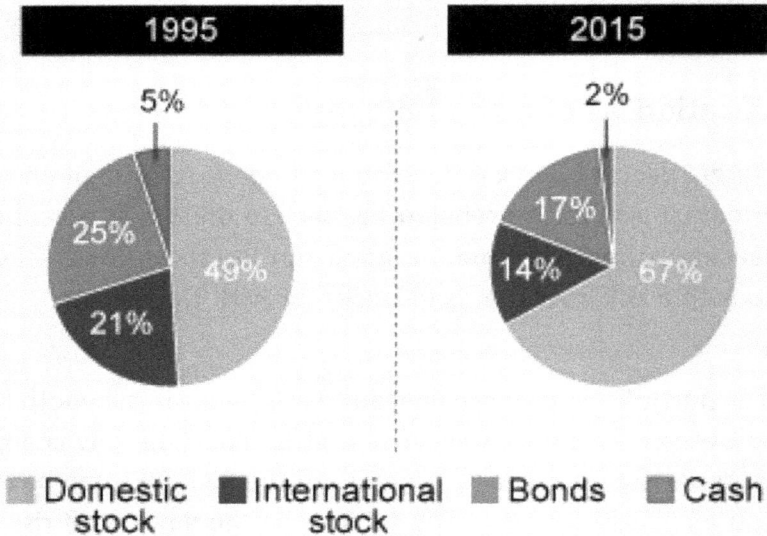

1995

5%

25%

21%

49%

2015

2%

17%

14%

67%

■ Domestic   ■ International   ■ Bonds   ■ Cash
   stock   stock

This chart's hypothetical illustration uses historical monthly performance from April 1995 through March 2015 from Morningstar/Ibbotson Associates; stocks are represented by the S&P 500 and MSCI EAFE Indexes, bonds are represented by Barclays U.S. Intermediate Government Treasury Bond Index, and short-term investments are represented by U.S. 30-day T-bills. Chart is for illustrative purposes only and is not indicative of any investment. Past performance is no guarantee of future results.

That extra stock meant the portfolio now had more potential risk. Why? Because while past performance does not guarantee future results, stocks have historically had larger price swings than bonds or cash. This means that when a portfolio skews toward stocks, the portfolio has the potential for bigger ups and downs. In fact, the portfolio's risk level as of May 2015 was nearly 10% greater than that of the target mix due to changes in the asset allocation associated with the relative returns to stocks, bonds, and cash.

Rebalancing is not just a risk-reducing exercise. The goal is to reset the investment mix to bring it back to the expected and appropriate risk level for the investor. Sometimes that means reducing risk by increasing the portion of a portfolio in more conservative options, but sometimes it means adding more risk to get back to the target mix. That could mean increasing investments in riskier asset classes such as stocks. Investing is an ongoing process.

An investor needs to create a plan, choose appropriate investments, and then conduct regular checkups to keep the portfolio on track.

- ✓ Review the portfolio on a quarterly basis. Regular review will keep an investor in touch with the individual positions in the portfolio and how it is doing relative to the stated goals.
- ✓ At a minimum Rebalancing should be done *once a year but twice a year* may be better.

Review the allocations and determine new target allocations within the ranges allowed under the investment policy. Consider:

- ✓ *The Point in the Business Cycle*
- ✓ *Any changes in risk tolerance*
- ✓ *Add to under allocations, subtract from over allocations.*

A great tool for evaluating an overall portfolio is Morningstar's XRAY analysis. It is available on their website or through Quicken.

When performing the review and rebalancing of the portfolio, create a buy/sell sheet. Enter the sell transactions for the account in the columns under "Sell" and enter the buy transactions for the account in the columns under "Buy". This documents the transactions making it easier to execute and also helps avoid mistakes.

A sample worksheet is provided below.

SELL TRANSACTIONS	ACCOUNT	TKR	Shares	$ AMOUNT	BUY TRANSACTIONS	ACCOUNT	TKR	Shares	$ AMOUNT
		Subtotal					Subtotal		
		Subtotal					Subtotal		
TOTAL SELL TRANSACTIONS . . .					TOTAL BUY TRANSACTIONS . . .				

The Power of Compounding

If an investor is patient and disciplined, money can grow and make a real difference in one's account balance over time.

The key is the power of compounding, the snowball effect that happens when earnings generate even more earnings. An investor receives interest not only on the original investments, but also on any interest, dividends, and capital gains that accumulate—so the money can grow faster and faster as the years roll on. This is particularly evident in retirement accounts, where principal is allowed to grow for years tax-deferred or even tax-free.

Here's an example:

Let's begin with two separate $10,000 investments that each earn 6% a year (this is a hypothetical example, and actual returns would likely be different). In one $10,000 investment, the investment earnings are withdrawn in cash each year, and the value of the account stays steady, the flat line in the chart below. In the other investment, the earnings are reinvested as shown by the curved line; this shows the power of compounding and time.

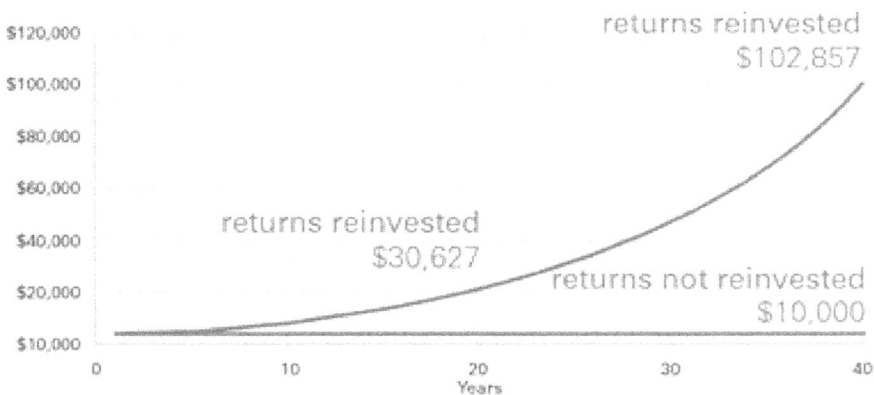

X
INVESTMENT POLICY

Putting it all together: Goals, risk tolerance, timeframe, asset allocation, diversification and rebalancing. Let's incorporated these elements into an *Investment Policy Statement (IPS)* personalized to the investor's individual unique needs

Every investor could potentially benefit from having an investment policy statement. It provides the foundation for all future investment decisions to be made by the investor. It serves as a guidepost, identifies goals and creates a systematic review process. The IPS is intended to keep investors focused on their objectives during short-term swings in the market and provides a baseline from which to monitor investment performance of the overall portfolio, as well as the performance of individual fund managers.

If a financial advisor's services are to be used, an IPS outlines the ground rules of the relationship between the investor and the advisor. The IPS is a reference to see whether or not the portfolio is achieving its stated goals and objectives. Any proposed changes to the investments may also be evaluated and reviewed against the overall objectives stated in the IPS.

A properly constructed Investment Policy Statement provides support for following a well-conceived, long-term investment discipline.

The investment Policy should:

> ➤ State the investor's major financial goals, either generally or specifically;
> ➤ Define risk tolerance and time horizon in enough detail for a third party to understand the investor's appetite for risk;
> ➤ Articulate an investment strategy whether it is a fixed allocation or a strategic allocation, or a different one of the investor's choosing;
> ➤ The portfolio allocation should be defined, including:
>   - The types of investments, asset classes and sub-classes in which the money will be invested,
>   - The percentage ranges of allocation to the investments choices,
>   - The percentage target allocations to the investments choices for the current investing period,
>   - The quality of the assets intended to be held in the portfolio.
> ➤ Monitoring and Rebalancing of the portfolio should be defined including the desired time frames to do so whether it is annual, semi-annual or quarterly.

The following table describes in more detail the elements of an Investment Policy Statement; the examples listed are for illustrative purposes in helping to describe the elements of the IPS.

EXAMPLES OF IPS ELEMENTS

Investment Objectives:	State your major financial goals, either generally or specifically. My primary financial objectives for my investment program were developed after a review of my financial resources, financial goals, asset allocation, risk tolerance and time horizon. My timeframe before my assets are needed is more than 10 years. • Objective 1: To retire at the age of 57 • Objective 2: To have an annual income from my investments of at least $50,000 after taxes and in today's dollars (inflation assumed to be 2.0 percent yearly) • Objective 3: To leave a meaningful inheritance for my children • Objective 4: To minimize potential tax liabilities
Risk Tolerance:	Define your Risk Tolerance in enough detail for a third party to understand your appetite for risk. ***MODERATE:*** *A Moderate investor values reducing risks and enhancing returns equally. This investor is willing to accept modest risks to seek higher long-term returns. A Moderate investor may endure a short-term loss of principal and lower degree of liquidity in exchange for long-term appreciation.* *I am willing to sacrifice some safety and accept some risk in exchange for higher returns and to stay ahead of inflation. I am **not** willing to take above average risk to achieve above average returns. I can tolerate negative returns from time to time.*
Strategy:	Articulate your Investment Strategy: Fixed, Strategic or other. A Fixed Allocation Strategy between Stocks and Fixed Income will be employed.

Portfolio Allocation:	Define the percentage allocation between Stocks and Fixed Income. The Allocation between stocks and fixed income will be: Stocks: 50% Fixed Income: 50%
Asset Allocation Ranges:	List the types of investments, asset classes and sub-classes in which you will invest your money; and the respective percentage ranges of allocation to each of them. **Stocks** and funds will be selected in the following asset sub-categories. To simplify rebalancing, the sub-allocations will be viewed separately totaling 100% of the stocks in the portfolio: • Large Capitalization U.S. Stocks 30-60% • Mid-Capitalization U S. Stocks 10-20% • Small Capitalization U S. Stocks 5-10% • International (non-U.S.) Company Stocks 10-25% • Emerging Market Stocks 0-5% • Individual Sector over-weighting 0-10% **Fixed Income** securities and funds will be selected in the following asset sub-categories. To simplify rebalancing, the sub-allocations will be viewed separately totaling 100% of the fixed income in the portfolio: • U.S. Treasury/Agency bills, notes, bonds & C.D.'s 20-80% • U.S. Corporate Bonds Investment Grade 20-50% • Treasury Inflation Protected Securities 0-20% • Municipal Bonds 0-35% • Closed-end Bond Funds 0-10% • Cash, Money Market, T-bills 5-25%

Target Allocation:	Define the percentage target allocations to the investments choices for the current investing period. **Stocks Allocation Target = 50%** <table><tr><td>• Large Capitalization U.S. Stocks: Growth</td><td>25%</td></tr><tr><td>• Large Capitalization U.S. Stocks: Value/Blend</td><td>30%</td></tr><tr><td>• Mid-Capitalization U S. Stocks</td><td>10%</td></tr><tr><td>• Small Capitalization U S. Stocks</td><td>5%</td></tr><tr><td>• International (non-U.S.) Company Stocks</td><td>20%</td></tr><tr><td>• Emerging Market Stocks</td><td>0%</td></tr><tr><td>• Individual Sector over-weighting</td><td><u>10%</u></td></tr><tr><td></td><td>100%</td></tr></table> **Fixed Income Allocation Target = 50%** <table><tr><td>• Cash, Money Market, T-bills, Short-term C.D.'s</td><td>15%</td></tr><tr><td>• U.S. Treasury/Agency, Notes, Bonds & C.D.'s</td><td>5%</td></tr><tr><td>• Treasury Inflation Protected Securities</td><td>0%</td></tr><tr><td>• Municipal Bonds: G.O. preferred</td><td>30%</td></tr><tr><td>• U.S. Corporate Bonds Investment Grade</td><td><u>50%</u></td></tr><tr><td></td><td>100%</td></tr></table>

Asset Quality:	The quality of the assets that you intend to hold in your portfolio. Funds invested herein shall generally conform to the following investment instruments and quality standards. Deviations from these quality standards shall be modest and apply to a small portion of the overall portfolio. **Stocks:** • Equity mutual funds with a Morningstar rating of four or five stars. • Equity Mutual Funds or ETFs may include Index Funds that track well known and broad indexes, for example, the Standards & Poor's Indexes. • U. S. Common Stocks: Morningstar and/or Standard & Poor's rating of three to five stars is preferred. A single stock should not exceed 5% of the portfolio allocation. • Foreign Stock utilizing the U.S. Depository Receipts (ADR's). **Bonds:** • Bond mutual funds and Exchange Traded Funds with a Morningstar rating of four or five stars; and invested in U.S. Government or investment grade corporate bonds and notes. • U.S. Government bonds, notes and bills. U.S. Agency Bonds. • Corporate bonds and notes with a Standard & Poor's rating of A- or better; or Moody's rating of A3 or better. • Municipal Bonds: Standard & Poor's rating of AA or better or Moody's equivalent. **Cash: (includes C.D.'s)** • Federally insured bank deposits by the FDIC. • Money market mutual funds at well-established fund companies.
Review and Rebalance	Monitoring and Rebalancing of the portfolio should be defined including the desired time frames to do so whether it is annual, semi-annual or quarterly. The plan for Review and Rebalancing the portfolio is to review the allocations twice a year. At that time new target allocations may be set for the portfolio within the ranges allowed under this policy.

A great deal of investing principles have been covered to this point. The Investment Policy Statement summarizes them relative to an investor's unique situation. It is important to take the time, make the appropriate decisions and document all the elements of a good investing plan for yourself into an IPS. After thoughtful reflection the plan should be completed and finalized.

The next two chapters discuss Brokerage accounts and Financial Professionals.

XI
BROKERAGE ACCOUNTS

Brokers make recommendations about specific investments like stocks, bonds, or mutual funds. While they may consider an investor's overall financial goals, brokers generally do not provide a detailed financial plan. Brokers are generally paid commissions when securities are bought or sold through them. When buying mutual funds from a broker make sure to ask questions about what fees are included in the mutual fund purchase. Brokerages vary widely in the quantity and quality of the services they provide for customers. Some have large research staffs, large national operations, and are prepared to service almost any kind of financial transaction an investor may need. Others are small and may specialize in promoting investments in unproven and very risky companies. And there's everything else in between.

A discount brokerage charges lower fees and commissions for its services than what would be paid at a full-service brokerage. But generally an investor has to research and choose investments themselves. If investments are self-directed a discount broker is a perfect match for the investor and the cost of the transactions is fairly low, approximately $8 to $10 each.

Below are a few discount brokers that are well known and provide good service.

- ➢ Charles Schwab
- ➢ Fidelity
- ➢ E*TRADE, and
- ➢ TD Ameritrade

There are many more brokerages: Most large mutual fund companies and Banks offer discount brokerage services. There are specialty firms that focus on option trades or other more esoteric products.

For investor's shopping for a discount brokerage account, it's pretty safe to pick one of the four discount brokers listed above.

Investors that need their portfolio managed and want all or most of the decisions made for them should look for a broker that offers this type of management; or a better choice would be engaging the services of a financial planner. See "Do you need a Financial Professional?" below.

Opening a Brokerage Account

When opening a brokerage account, whether in person or online, an investor will typically be asked to sign a new account agreement. It is important to carefully review all the information in this agreement because it determines the investor's legal rights regarding the brokerage account.

Some do's and don'ts:

- ✓ Do not sign the new account agreement unless you thoroughly understand it and agree with the terms and conditions it imposes on you.
- ✓ Do not rely on statements about your account that are not in the agreement.
- ✓ Ask for a copy of any account documentation prepared for you by the broker.

The broker should ask an investor about their investment goals and personal financial situation, including one's income, net worth, investment experience, and how much risk the investor is willing to take on. The broker relies on this information to determine which investments will best meet the investment goals and tolerance for risk.

If a broker tries to sell an investment before asking these questions, that's a very bad sign. It signals that the broker has a greater interest in earning a commission than recommending an investment that meets the needs of the investor.

Generally a new account agreement requires that an investor make three critical decisions:

Who will make the final decisions about what you buy and sell in your account?

The account owner will have the final say on investment decisions unless "discretionary authority" is given to the broker. Discretionary authority allows the broker to invest money in the brokerage account without consulting the owner about the price, the type of security, the amount, and when to buy or sell. Do not give discretionary authority to a broker without seriously considering the risks involved in turning control of your money over to another person.

How much risk should you assume?

In a new account agreement, the account owner must specify their overall investment objective in terms of risk. Categories of risk may have labels such as "income," "growth," or "aggressive growth." Be certain to fully understand the distinctions among these terms, and be certain that the risk level chosen accurately reflects one's age, experience and investment goals. Be sure that the investment products recommended by the broker reflect the category of risk that has been selected.

Arbitration: When opening a new account, the brokerage firm may ask that a legally binding contract to use the arbitration process to settle any future dispute between you and the firm or sales representative is signed. Signing this agreement means that you give up the right to sue the sales representative and firm in court.

XII
FINANCIAL PROFESSIONALS

Do You need a Financial Professional?

Depending on how busy your life is with other responsibilities: your job, children, etc.; or if you feel that you don't know enough about investing on your own, then you may need professional investment advice. Investment professionals offer a variety of services at a variety of prices. It pays to comparison shop. You can get investment advice from most financial institutions that sell investments, including brokerages, banks, mutual funds, and insurance companies. You can also hire a broker, an investment adviser, an accountant, a financial planner, or other professional to help you make investment decisions.

Investment Advisers and Financial Planners

Some financial planners and investment advisers offer a complete financial plan, assessing every aspect of a client's financial life and developing a detailed strategy for meeting their financial goals. They may charge a fee for the plan, a percentage of the assets that they manage, or receive commissions from the companies whose products are bought; or a combination of these. It is important to know exactly what services are provided and how much they will cost.

An investment professional has a duty to make sure that he or she only recommends investments that are suitable for their client. That is, that the investment makes sense based on the client's other securities holdings, financial situation, means, and any other information that the investment professional thinks is important.

People or firms that get paid to give advice about investing in securities generally must register with either the SEC or the state securities agency where they have their principal place of business. *Federal and state law requires that Registered Investment Advisors (RIA) be held to a Fiduciary Standard.* This requires an advisor to act solely in the best interest of the client at all times. RIAs must disclose any conflict, or potential conflict, to the client prior to and throughout a business engagement and must adopt a Code of Ethics and fully disclose how they are compensated.

Unfortunately, only a small proportion of "financial advisors" are federally or state-registered RIAs. Most so-called financial advisors are considered "Broker-Dealers" by the Securities and Exchange Commission (SEC). Brokers are not held to a Fiduciary Standard; they are held to the lower Suitability Standard. In fact, they are required by federal law to act in the best interest of their employer, not in the best interest of their clients.

Under the Dodd-Frank Wall Street Reform and Consumer Protection Act (Dodd-Frank Act), the SEC was given the authority to — but is not required to — adopt a uniform fiduciary standard of conduct for both broker-dealers and registered investment advisers when providing financial advice to retail customers. The SEC is in the process of determining its rules regarding this subject. The notice of proposed rulemaking for the Personalized Investment Advice Standard of Conduct is expected in October 2016, but this is subject to change.

To find out about advisers and whether they are properly registered, read their registration forms, called the "Form ADV." The Form ADV has two parts. Part 1 has information about the adviser's business and whether they've had problems with regulators or clients. Part 2 outlines the adviser's services, fees, and strategies. Before hiring an investment adviser, always ask for and carefully read both parts of the ADV. An adviser's most recent Form ADV may be viewed online by visiting the Investment Adviser Public Disclosure (IAPD) website at http://www.adviserinfo.sec.gov/IAPD/Default.aspx.

Compensation Models

To use a cliché, "there is no such thing as a free lunch". Professional financial advisers usually do not perform their services pro bono. If they are working for a client, they are getting paid for their efforts. Some of their fees are more obvious or disclosed more clearly. But feel free to ask questions about how and how much the adviser is being paid.

Be sure that you understand the various ways in which a financial professional can be compensated. How compensation is received may affect the advice you receive, if that planner faces hidden conflicts of interest. If the fee is quoted as a percentage, it is important to understand what that translates to in dollars. The three most common models of compensation are:

➢ **Fee-Only Compensation:** This model minimizes conflicts of interest. A Fee-Only financial advisor charges the client directly for his or her advice and/or ongoing management. No other financial reward is provided by any institution—which means that the advisor does not receive commissions on the actions they take on the clients' behalf. Compensation is based on an hourly rate, a percent of assets managed, a flat fee, or a retainer. This is the required form of compensation for members of NAPFA.

➢ **Fee-Based Compensation (fee and commission):** This form is often confused with Fee-Only, but it's not the same. Fee-based advisors charge clients a fee for the advice delivered, but they also sometimes receive payments for products they sell or recommend. In some cases, commissions are credited towards the fee, giving the appearance of a lower-priced option. Any outside compensation lessens the advisor's ability to keep the client's best interests first and foremost.

➢ **Commissions:** Advisors are compensated for the sale of investments, insurance, or other financial products. The compensation is paid by the firm providing the products, usually a mutual fund company or insurance company. NAPFA has always maintained that an advisor who is compensated through commissions is primarily a salesperson. A client working with a commissioned sales person must always ask himself: Is this advice truly in my best interest, or is it the most profitable product for the advisor? In fact, a commissioned advisor usually is required to put the best interests of his employer ahead of the best interests of his client.

In summary, there are more than 100 professional designations in the financial planning industry, but only a few of them truly indicate a professional's ability to do real broad based financial planning. Some are more appropriate for institutional investing than the consumer; others are specific to the insurance industry. FINRA has a list of accredited designations.

The National Association of Personal Financial Advisors (NAPFA) suggests looking for financial advisors who have one or more of the following designations:

➢ *Certified Financial Planner™ (CFP®)*

➢ *Personal Financial Specialist (CPA/PFS) – granted to CPAs who meet necessary requirements*

➢ *Chartered Financial Consultant (ChFC)*

CONCLUSION

I hope you are energized and ready to get started. The road in front of you should be clear. There may be a few twists and turns, but you should be ready to navigate them.

It is important to be realistic in your expectations for market returns. The investment plan that you are creating, as this writing is guiding you to do, will develop a portfolio risk profile in line with your risk tolerance and stage of life. Your performance will be appropriately geared; you will gain confidence; you will stick with the plan and over time you will fulfill your goals and live a very happy financial life.

Conversely, if your expectations are too great, your portfolio will likely underperform those expectations. This may encourage you to take on more risk to try to achieve the greater returns. This is a potentially dangerous situation.

An investing plan removes emotion from the process. It makes investing a business. The following list is a review of the steps to constructing an investing plan:

- ✓ Define your Goals
- ✓ Determine your Timeframe
- ✓ Document your Financial Position and Cash Flows
- ✓ Determine your Risk Tolerance
- ✓ Determine an appropriate Asset Allocation to major asset classes and sub-classes
- ✓ Determine a methodology for Selecting investments
- ✓ Determine how you will Monitor your portfolio & Rebalance it
- ✓ Write and Investment Policy Statement

A complete model Investment Policy Statement is provided at the end of this book, following the Glossary. It is provided as a starting point to help with the construction of this important document. It should be tailored to your specific situation; especially the risk tolerance, asset allocations and asset quality sections.

As you implement your investing plan and monitor its performance, the following points are provided to reflect upon at each review session:

➢ Risk is for the equity (stock) allocation, never violate the set asset quality for fixed income securities. Bonds, CD's and cash stabilize the portfolio and gets an investor through the rough times.

➢ Stay diversified, if it is desirable to emphasize a particular sector or individual stock, do so within the sector allocation percentage specified in the IPS.

➢ Watch the business cycles and market valuations. They will provide tips that times may be changing. If the Strategic Asset Allocation strategy is being used, this is what will be the yardstick to determine it is time to change the portfolio allocation.

➢ Don't get greedy or scared, stick to the investing plan it helps maintain discipline.

➢ If a particular investment is not performing well or as expected, reevaluate its place in the portfolio. Does it still belong?

There have been many techniques to investing past and present, but when one steps back and considers the sage advice of the many notables – Benjamin Graham, Sir John Templeton, Peter Lynch, John Bogle, Jesse Livermore, Warren Buffet and Charlie Munger -- it generally boils down to:

- ✓ Picking good companies to invest money in, and
- ✓ Buy them at a fair price, then
- ✓ Holding them for periods of time to allow for the growth of the money.

Remember, investing is for the long haul. As Buffett once said, "Our favorite holding period is forever".

Good luck with your investment plan and success to you in the financial markets!

NOTES

1. Reference Securities and Exchange Commission publication "Saving and Investing, A Roadmap to your journey to Financial Security".

2. Risk Tolerance, market fluctuations: J.P. Morgan Guide to the Markets as of Dec. 31 2015.

3. Risk Tolerance Classification Definitions: Stifel, Nicolaus & Company, Inc.

4. Stocks and Bonds: FINRA

5. Rating Agencies: Morningstar, Inc.; Standard & Poor's, Inc.: S&P Capital IQ

6. Rating Agencies for Bonds: Wikipedia "Bond Credit Rating"

7. Business Cycles: Economics.about.com; reference: Parkin and Bade text "Economics".

8. Allocation: Benjamin Graham Rule of Thumb Quote. Bogleheads.com; Graham, Benjamin. *The Intelligent Investor* (2003 edition annotated by Jason Zweig ed.).

9. Allocation: John Bogle Rule of Thumb Quote. Bogleheads.com; 2010 edition of *Common Sense on Mutual Funds*, pp.87-88

10. Asset Class Returns: The Vanguard Group, Inc.

11. Asset Allocations Examples: Fidelity Investments.

12. Diversification: Fidelity Viewpoints 08/19/2015 "The pro's guide to diversification".

13. Diversification Asset Categories: Investopedia

14. Diversification Sectors: Wikipedia: Global Industry Classification Standard (GICS) is an industry taxonomy developed in 1999 by MSCI and Standard & Poor's (S&P)

15. Diversification: Non U.S. equities; Vanguard research

16. Diversification: Correlation to market segments; Vanguard

17. Rebalancing: Fidelity Viewpoints 08/19/2015 "The pro's guide to diversification".

18. Power of Compounding: The Vanguard Group, Inc.

19. Financial Professionals: RIA Fiduciary Standard; NAPFA "Pursuit of a Financial Advisor"

20. Financial Professionals: Compensation Models; NAPFA "Pursuit of a Financial Advisor"

21. Financial Professionals: Credentials; NAPFA "Pursuit of a Financial Advisor"

22. Financial Professionals: Professional Designations; Mark P. Cussen, CFP®, CMFC, AFC "A Guide to Financial Designations"

23. Glossary of Terms: Stock Market Briefing.com

GLOSSARY OF INVESTING TERMS

Comprehensive listing of Stock Market terms and terminology

- A -

Accrued Interest: Interest due from last coupon date to present on an interest bearing security. Buyer of security pays the quoted price plus accrued interest.

ADR: American Depositary Receipt. A tool for allowing American investors to buy shares of foreign-based corporations in the U.S. rather than in overseas markets. ADRs are receipts for the shares of a foreign-based corporation held in the vault of a U.S. bank which entitles the shareholders to all dividends and capital gains. ADS (American Depository Share - a term often used interchangeably with ADR) is the share representing the underlying ordinary share which trades in the issuer's home market. Technically, ADS is the instrument which actually trades, while ADR is the certificate that represents a number of ADSs.

Advance-Decline (A/D) Line: is a measurement of market breadth. It is calculated by subtracting the number of stocks that decline in price over a given period (weekly or daily) from the number that advance, and accumulating the differences. When advancing issues outnumber declining issues, the A/D line moves upward. Conversely, if the majority of issues fall in price the line trends downward. The basic calculation should be adjusted slightly to facilitate historical comparability. Each week (assuming a weekly A/D line) divide the difference of advances minus declines by the total number of issues changing in price. For example, if there were 6000 advancers and 4000 decliners the ratio would be (6000-4000)/10,000, or 0.20. Then accumulate the weekly ratio readings. Without this adjustment the A/D line exhibits a bullish bias given the long-term increase in the number of issues traded. When this adjusted A/D line is in a uptrend, the odds are that stocks are in a bull market. If the adjusted A/D line is falling, the likelihood of a major downtrend increases. The A/D line is in an established uptrend when the current weekly figure is above the average A/D line reading of the last 52-weeks. A downtrend is established when the current A/D line reading is below the average A/D line reading of the last 52-wks.

Agencies: Federal agency securities, i.e. FNMA, GNMA.

Amortization: An accounting method that allows a company to write-off intangible rights or assets over the period of their existence.

Annual Report: A firm's annual statement of operating and financial results. It contains an income statement, a balance sheet, a statement of changes in financial position, an auditor's report and a summary of operations.

Arbitrage: The simultaneous purchase and sale of substantially identical assets in order to profit from a price difference between the two assets.

Averaging Down: Buying shares of the same security at successively lower prices in order to reduce the average purchasing price.

- B -

Balance Sheet: The summary of a company's assets, liabilities, and shareholders' equity. Since balance sheets do not list items at their current monetary value, they may overstate or understate the real value of certain corporate assets and liabilities. Also called the statement of financial condition.

Basis: The spread between a bond futures price and the cash price of a bond deliverable to the bond futures contract.

Basis Point: One one-hundredth of one percent (1/100 of 1%).

Bear Market: An extended period of general price declines in an individual security or other asset.

Beige Book: A Federal Reserve report on economic conditions released roughly two weeks prior to each FOMC meeting. The report is compiled by the 12 Fed district banks based primarily on anecdotal information. The Fed does not place much emphasis on the Beige Book when making policy decisions; more emphasis is placed on the Blue and Green Books, which are only made available to FOMC members.

Big Board: The New York Stock Exchange.

Block Trade: A trade of 10,000 shares or more.

Blue Chip Stocks: Nationally known companies which usually have large-capitalizations and long records of profitable growth and dividend payments. Examples include General Motors, 3M, Coca Cola, and IBM. Blue chip stocks are generally considered less risky than small-cap companies but have less potential for large short-term gains.

Blue Sky Laws: State regulations covering the offering and sale of securities within state boundaries.

Bond Equivalent Yield: Annual yield on a short term, non-interest bearing security calculated so as to be comparable to yields of interest-bearing securities.

Book Value: Book Value is often used as an indicator for selecting undervalued stocks. It is also used to determine the ultimate value of securities in a liquidation. Book value is calculated by the following: Total assets minus intangible assets (goodwill, patents, etc.) minus any long-term liabilities EQUALS total net assets. This figure, divided by the number of shares of preferred and/or common stock, gives the Net Asset Value - or Book Value - per share of preferred or common stock.

Breadth of the Market: The percentage of stocks participating in a particular market move. If two thirds of the stocks listed on an exchange rise during a given trading day, it is generally considered good breadth. Analysts look to this as an indicator that the trend is probably more significant and longer-lasting than one with limited breadth.

Breakout: The advance of a stock price above a resistance level, or the fall of a stock price below a support level. If a stock experiences a breakout on heavy volume, it indicates to market technicians that the stock is about to engage in a major price move in the direction of the breakout.

Bull Market: An extended period of generally rising prices in an individual item (a stock), group of items (an industry group), or the market as a whole.

- C -

CAGR: Compound Annual Growth Rate.

Call Option: An option that permits the owner (option holder) to purchase a specific asset at a predetermined price until a certain date.

Callable Bond: A bond which the issuer may redeem prior to maturity by paying a stated call price.

Capitalization: A term usually referring to Market Capitalization which is the value of a company as determined by the most recent stock price multiplied by the number of shares outstanding.

Cash Flow: Cash flow is an important aspect of a company's performance. It is an analysis of all the changes affecting cash in the categories of operations, investments, and financing. A positive cash flow means that more cash is taken in than is paid out, and the opposite is a negative cash flow. A company might be forced into bankruptcy, even with assets well in excess of liabilities, if it does not have enough cash to meet current obligations.

Cash Market: In the Treasury market, this term refers to trading in Treasuries for immediate delivery, as opposed to the futures market, where securities are traded for future delivery.

CBOE: Chicago Board Options Exchange.

CBT: Chicago Board of Trade.

Certificate of Deposit (CD): A time deposit with a specific maturity.

Common Stock: Often called Capital Stock, it is units of ownership in a public corporation which typically entitles the holder to vote on the selection of directors and receive dividends. In the event of a liquidation, claims of secured and unsecured creditors and bond and preferred stock holders take precedence over common stock holders.

Competitive Bid: Bid submitted at a Treasury auction for a specific amount of securities at a specific price.

Coupon: The annual rate of interest on a bond's face value that the issuer must pay to the holder of the bond.

CPI: Consumer Price Index.

CPI-Indexed Treasury Notes (or TIPS): Treasury issues which protect the investor from inflation as determined by the CPI.

Current Yield: A measure of an investor's return on a bond calculated by dividing the annual interest on the bond by the market price. It is the actual income rate or the yield to maturity as opposed to the coupon rate (the two would be the same if a bond was purchased at par). For example, a 10% (coupon rate) bond with a face value (par) of $1000 is bought at a market price of $800. The annual income on the bond is $100, but since $800 was paid for the bond, the current yield is $100 divided by $800 or 12 1/2%.

Curve: See Yield Curve.

- D -

Dealer: A dealer acts as a principal in all transaction, both buying and selling for its own account.

Debt to Asset Ratio: A coverage ratio that measures the amount of debt a company has in relation to its assets. It is calculated by dividing Total Debt by Total Assets. The amount of Debt to Asset may vary from industry to industry and should be compared as such.

Debt to Equity Ratio: A measurement of financial leverage - the use of borrowed money to enhance the return on owner's equity. It is calculated by Long-Term Debt divided by Common Stockholders Equity. The higher the ratio, the greater the leverage.

Depreciation: An accounting method to amortize fixed assets, such as plant and equipment, so as to allocate the cost over their depreciable life. Depreciation reduces taxable income but does not reduce cash. The most common methods are accelerated depreciation and straight-line depreciation.

Derivative: A financial instrument whose value is based on the performance of an underlying financial asset, index, or other investment. For example, as Option is a derivative because its value changes in relation to the performance of an underlying stock.

Devaluation: The lowering of the value of a country's currency relative to gold and/or the currencies of other nations. When a currency is devalued, imported goods become more expensive, while its exports become less expensive.

Discount Basis: Yield basis on which short term securities are quoted. Treasury bills are typically quoted on a discount basis, which understates their return relative to notes and bond.

Discount Rate: The interest rate that the Federal Reserve charges member banks for loans, using government securities as collateral. This provides a floor for interest rates since banks set their loan rates a notch above the discount rate. The discount rate is also used in determining the Present Value of future Cash Flows.

Dividends: A distribution of a company's earnings to shareholders prorated by class of security and usually paid in the form of cash or stock. The amount is decided by the Board of Directors and is usually paid quarterly.

Duration: A measure of current maturity of a fixed income security as the weighted average of the time to receipt of the instrument's payments - the weights are the present values of the future payments.

- E -

Earnings: A term generalized term referring to corporate profits. Profits can be calculated in different ways depending upon the industry and accounting practices. Earnings is one of the frequently used measures of a company's financial condition. It is commonly used to determine the risk/reward profile of a given security - the ratio of stock price to earnings (see P/E Ratio).

Earnings per Share: The dollars of profit generated for each share of common stock. A company that earned $1 million last year and has 1 million shares outstanding would report earnings per share of $1.00. The figure is calculated after paying taxes, preferred shareholders and bond holders.

EBITA: Earnings before interest, taxes, and amortization

EBITDA: Earnings before interest, taxes, depreciation, and amortization

ECB: European Central Bank. The central bank for the European Monetary Union.

Effective Date: In the securities industry, it is the date when an offering filed with the Securities and Exchange Commission may commence - usually 20 days after the filing of the registration statement.

EU: European Union. A group of fifteen European nations that cooperate on trade and fiscal policy decisions. The fifteen members are: Austria, Belgium, Denmark, Finland, France, Germany, Greece, Ireland, Italy, Luxembourg, Netherlands, Portugal, Spain, Sweden, United Kingdom.

Euro: The common currency of the European Monetary Union.

- F -

Fannie Mae: (Federal National Mortgage Association) Publicly owned, government-sponsored corporation, established in 1938 to purchase both government-backed and conventional mortgages from lenders and securitize them. Its objective is to increase the affordability of home mortgage funds for low to middle income home buyers. It is the largest source of home mortgage funds in the U.S. and a large issuer of debt securities which are used to finance it activities. Equity shares of Fannie Mae trade on the NYSE.

FASB: Financial Accounting Standards Board.

Federal Funds Rate: The interest rate banks charge on overnight loans to other banks in need of funds in order to meet reserve requirements. The rate is set by the Federal Reserve.

Fixed Exchange Rate: A set rate of exchange between currencies determined by agreement.

Float: The difference between the credits given by the Fed to banks' accounts on checks being cleared through the Fed and debits made to the banks' accounts on the same checks. Increased float (which can occur due to bad weather and transportation problems) adds liquidity to the banking system.

Floating Exchange Rate: Rates determined by the response of the currencies to market forces.

FOMC: Federal Open Market Committee. Comprised of the seven members of the Board of Governors, the President of the NY Fed, and four other Fed district bank presidents on a rotating basis. Meets eight times each year to set monetary policy.

Foreign Exchange Rate: The price at which one currency trades for another.

Foreign Exchange Risk: The risk that a long or short position in a foreign security may be adversely affected by a change in the value of the foreign currency.

Futures Contract: An agreement to buy or sell a specific amount of a commodity or financial instrument at a particular price on a stipulated date.

The price is established between the buyer and seller on the floor of an exchange. A contract obligates the buyer to purchase an underlying commodity and the seller to sell it, unless the contract is sold to another before the settlement date. This contrasts with options trading, in which the option buyer may choose whether or not to exercise the option by the exercise date.

- G -

GAAP: Generally Accepting Accounting Procedures.

Goodwill: In accounting, goodwill is any advantage, such as brand names, that enables a business to earn higher profits than its competitors.

Gross Domestic Product (GDP): GDP is the total value of goods and services produced by a nation.

Gross Margin: A measure calculated by dividing gross profit (net sales minus cost of goods sold) by net sales.

Gross National Product: GNP is the dollar value of all goods and services produced in a nation's economy, including goods and services produced abroad.

Growth Stock: Stock of a corporation that has exhibited faster-than-average gains in earnings over the last few years and is expected to continue to show high levels of profit growth. Over the long run, growth stocks tend to outperform slower-growing stocks but they also tend to have higher price/earnings ratios and are consequently, riskier investments.

- H -

Hedge Fund: Investment vehicles, much like mutual funds, which are generally structured as partnerships wherein the number of investors is limited and whose general partner has made a substantial personal investment in the fund. The offering memorandum of most Hedge Funds allows them to use a combination of sophisticated investment strategies such as taking both long and short positions, using leverage and derivatives, and investing in many markets. The funds usually require investors to make a large fixed investment (i.e. $100,000) and only allows withdrawals at certain times of the year. Because Hedge Funds move billions of dollars in and out of markets quickly, they can have a significant impact on the day-to-day trading developments in the stock, bond, and futures markets.

Hedging: Hedging is an investment strategy most often used to offset potential risk, although it can be used as a speculative investment in and of itself. Widely used hedging techniques include buying or selling Put or Call Options, Selling Short, and buying or selling the Futures market. (See Options)

- I -

Indexes - Domestic: An Index is a statistical composite that is used to indicate the performance of a market or a market sector over various time periods. The following is a variety of indices that are used to gauge the performance of stocks and other securities in the U.S.

- *Amex Index*: Composite index of shares listed on the American Stock Exchange.

- *Arms Index:* Also known as the short-term trading index, is the average volume of declining issues divided by the average volume of advancing issues.

- *Barclays Capital U.S. Aggregate Bond Index:* The index measures the performance of the U.S. investment grade bond market. The index invests in a wide spectrum of public, investment-grade, taxable, fixed income securities in the United States – including government, corporate, and international dollar-denominated bonds, as well as mortgage-backed and asset-backed securities, all with maturities of more than 1 year.; formerly known as Lehman Brothers Aggregate Bond Index.

- *Barclays Capital U.S. Treasury Bond Index:* An index of prices of treasury bonds with remaining maturities of one year or more; formerly known as Lehman Brothers Treasury Bond Index.

- *Dow Jones Industrial Average:* The best known of all U.S. stock indices, the Dow as it is often called, contains 30 stocks that trade on the NYSE (New York Stock Exchange) and is a general indicator of how shares of the largest U.S. companies are trading.

- *Dow Jones Transportation Average:* The DJIA monitors the stock performance of 20 airlines, railroads, and trucking companies.

- *Dow Jones Utility Average*: The DJUA monitors the stock performance of 15 gas, electric, and power companies.

- *Dow Jones Composite Average*: Tracks the stock performance of the 65 stocks which comprise the three averages listed above.

- *NASDAQ Composite Index:* A composite index of more than 3000 companies listed on the NASDAQ (also referred to as over-the-counter or OTC stocks). It is designed to indicate the stock performance of small-cap and technology stocks.

- *New York Stock Exchange Composite Index:* A composite index of shares listed on the NYSE.

- *Russell 2000 Index:* A market capitalization weighted index published by Frank Russell of Tacoma Washington, the Russell 2000 is one of the most widely regarded measures of the stock price performance of small companies. It is a part of the Russell 3000 Index consists of the 3000 largest U.S. stocks in terms of market capitalization. The highest-ranking 1000 stocks are in the Russell 1000 Index (which closely mirrors the S&P % Index). The remaining 2000 stocks, the Russell 2000 Index, represent approximately 11% of the Russell 3000 Index's total market capitalization.

- *S&P 500 Index:* A broad-based measurement of changes in stock market conditions based on the average performance of 500 widely held stocks including industrial, transportation, financial, and utility stocks. The composition of the 500 stocks is flexible and the number of issues in each sector varies over time.

- *Value Line Composite Index:* An equal-weighted index which averages the price change from the previous day's close in each of the index's approximately 1700 component stocks. Smaller, more volatile stocks have the same impact on the index value as large-cap less volatile stocks, therefore, the index is more sensitive to economic changes than a broad-based index.

- *Wilshire 5000 Index:* A widely-watched "total market" index that attempts to track the direction of most of the widely-traded shares on U.S. exchanges including small-, mid-, and large-cap issues.

Indexes - International:

- CAC 40: Paris

- DAX 30: Frankfurt

- FT-SE 100: London

- Hang Seng: Hong Kong

- Nikkei 225: Tokyo

Initial Public Offering: Corporations first offering of stock to the public. The share prices of IPOs can fluctuate wildly, with what seems to be little regard for the current value of the underlying company.

Insider Trading: Refers to both the legal trading by corporate officers based on public information and illegal trading by anyone of securities from information not available to the public.

Institutional Investors: Holdings by organization that trade large volumes of securities such as banks, mutual funds, insurance companies, pension funds, college endowment funds, etc.

Interest Sensitive Stock: Stock of a company whose earnings change when interest rates move, such as a bank or utility. These stocks tend to go up or down on news of interest rate changes.

- J - K - L -

Junk Bonds: High risk bonds with low credit ratings.

LIBOR: London Interbank Offered Rate - rate that the most creditworthy international banks dealing in Eurodollars charge each other for large loans. It is usually a basis for other large Eurodollar loans to less creditworthy corporate and government borrowers. For example, a Third World country may have to pay a point over LIBOR when it borrows money.

- M -

Margin Account: A brokerage account allowing customers to buy securities with money borrowed from the brokerage firm. Margin accounts are governed by Regulation T, the NASD, the NYSE, and the firm's house rules. Margin requirements can be met with cash or eligible securities. Under Federal Reserve Board regulation, the initial margin required since 1945 has ranged from 50 to 100 percent of the security's purchase price.

Mark to Market: The process of daily revaluation of a security to reflect its current market value instead of its acquisition price or book value.

Market Value: For purposes of the securities industry, market value is the current market price of a security - as indicated by the latest trade recorded.

MBS: Mortgage Backed Security; such as FNMAs, GNMAs.

Momentum Investing: An investment style that is currently popular among investors. It involves targeting companies with rapidly growing earnings - i.e. a history of positive quarterly earnings surprises. The strategy inevitably involves buying stocks with extremely high P/E ratios and carries a great deal of risk. Momentum investing is favored by aggressive managers of aggressive growth and capital appreciation mutual funds.

Money Center Bank: The largest U.S. banks (mostly in New York) which play an important role in the markets.

Money Market: Market in which short term debt instruments are traded.

Mortgage Backed Securities: Debt issues backed by a pool of mortgages. Investors receive payments from the interest and principal payment to the underlying mortgages.

Moving Average: A tool used in technical analysis and charts. It is the average prices of securities or commodities constructed over a given period and showing trends for the latest interval. For example, a thirty-day moving average includes yesterday's figures; tomorrow the same average will include today's figures and will no longer show those for the earliest date included in the average. Thus, every day the average includes figures for the latest day and drops figures for the earliest day.

Municipals: Securities issued by state and local governments or their agencies.

Mutual Fund: A fund operated by an investment company that pools money from shareholders and invests in various instruments such as stocks, bonds, options, futures, currencies, or money market securities. Mutual funds vary in their focus - some invest solely in foreign securities, some target capital appreciation, while others invest to generate income. Investors in mutual funds can more easily diversify their holdings and take advantage of a professional management team. Investors can expect to pay management fees for the service.

- N -

NASDAQ: National Association of Securities Dealers Automated Quotations. The Nasdaq National Market is comprised of over 3,000 companies whose shares trade via a computerized system that provides brokers and dealers with price quotes. While companies have to meet certain requirements to be listed on the Nasdaq; Nasdaq stocks are usually small-cap companies without long histories of earnings and tend to be more volatile.

NAV: Net Asset Value.

New York Stock Exchange: Founded in 1792, the NYSE is the oldest and largest stock exchange in the U.S. The Big Board, as it is known, lists more than 1,600 companies who meet stringent listing requirements. There are 1.366 seats on the NYSE, many of which are owned by partners or officers of securities firms, and which handle trades for the public.

- O -

Open Market Operation: One of the three means of conducting Monetary Policy used by the Federal Reserve. It involves the purchase and sale of government securities by the Federal Reserve Bank of New York (as directed by the Federal Open Market Committee) in an effort to regulate the money supply. The actions of the New York Fed effectively alter bank reserves which, in turn, effects the supply of credit. This effect is realized throughout the economy.

Operating Income: Essentially, it is the income derived from a company's regular business, excluding all income or losses from other sources. Operating income is defined as the revenues of a business minus related costs and expenses. It excludes extraordinary items such as, all realized gains and losses on investments or discontinued operations, taxes, prior year adjustments, write-offs of intangibles, bonuses and other profit distributions to employees, sales of divisions, etc.

Options: The right to buy or sell stock at a certain price before a specified date. If the buyer chooses not to exercise the option, the option expires and the option buyer forfeits the money.

Over-the-Counter Stocks: Stocks that are not listed and do not trade on an organized exchange, such as the NYSE or the AMEX. They are usually small-cap companies that do not meet the exchange requirements. Trading procedures are written and enforced by the National Association of Securities Dealers (NASD), a self-regulatory group. Transactions are conducted by phone and computer network which connects dealers and provides quotes. Some large companies (i.e. Intel and Microsoft) have chosen to remain as over-the-counter because they favor the system of multiple trading by many dealers over the centralized exchange system of specialists.

- P - Q –

Par: The nominal or face values of a security. Bonds are issued at and mature at par which is usually $1000 per bond. Prior to maturity, they trade at, above or below par, depending on their coupon rate versus the current level of interest rates. Par value for Common Stocks is set by the issuing company and has no relation to market value. Par value is more important in the case of Preferred Stock, where dividends are often stated as a percentage of the par value of the preferred stock issue.

Pass-through: A mortgage-backed security on which payment of interest and principal on the underlying mortgages is passed through to the bondholder.

PEG: A valuation measure which compares the P/E ratio of a company to its earnings growth rate (Price/Earnings to Growth, hence PEG). The P/E and earnings growth rates used can be either trailing numbers or forward estimates.

PPI: Producer Price Index.

Preferred Shares: A class of stock that normally pays dividends at a fixed rate and carries no voting rights. Preferred shareholders do, however, carry a preference over shareholders of Common Stock in the payment of dividends and liquidation of assets.

Premium: The amount by which the price at which an issue is trading or is auctioned exceeds the par value of the issue.

Present Value: The current value of a future payment given an appropriate interest rate assumption.

Price/Earnings Ratio (P/E): A widely used valuation measure of the relationship between a stock's price and its earnings per share, it is also referred to as Multiple to Earnings or simply, The Multiple. Its formula is: current stock price per share divided by the most current earnings per share. It is an important tool for investors as it indicates how much they are paying for a company's earning power. Stocks with low P/E multiples (those below 20, although relative multiples do vary from industry to industry) tend to be slow growth, steady and perhaps mature companies. Those with higher P/E multiples are usually growth stocks and tend be more risky. Trailing P/E multiples use last year's earnings and the current price.

Price to Book Value: Also called Multiple to Book Value, it is a measure of the relative risk/reward profile of a stock. It is calculated by dividing the latest stock price per share by the most recent per share value of stockholders equity (book value). A company with a stock price of $12 per share and a book value of $6 per share is trading at two times book value. Generally, the higher the multiple to book value, the riskier the stock is, however, it is important to know that multiples vary from industry to industry and should be considered as such.

Prime Rate: The interest rate at which banks lend to their best customers.

Principal: The face amount or par value of a security.

Put Option: An option that gives the owner (option holder) the right, but not the obligation, to sell a specific asset at a predetermined price until a certain date. Investors purchase put options in order to take advantage of a decline in the price of the asset.

- R -

Ratings: An evaluation of a security's credit-worthiness by Moody's, Standard & Poor's, or other credit rating agencies.

Real Interest Rates: Nominal interest rates less the expected rate of inflation.

Refunding: Redemption of securities by funds raised through the sale of a new issue. In the Treasury market, the refunding typically refers to the quarterly auctions at which the Treasury sells 5, 10, and 30-year notes and bonds.

REIT: Real Estate Investment Trust. Publicly traded companies that manage portfolios of real estate to generate profits. The underlying assets are investments in shopping centers, medical facilities, office buildings apartment complexes, hotels, and various other real estate holdings. One type of REIT take equity positions in real estate and distribute the income from rents and capital gains (when properties are sold) to shareholders. Other REITs act as lenders to property developers and pass interest income on to shareholders. A third type of REIT combines equity and mortgage investments. To avoid taxation, REITs must distribute 95% of their taxable income to shareholders annually.

Repo or Repurchase Agreement: A holder of securities sells securities to another party with an agreement to repurchase the securities on a set date for a set price. The security seller is essentially borrowing money from the buyer. When the Fed conducts repos or RPs, it is buying securities with an agreement to resell them at a later date. The Fed is thus adding reserves to the banking system temporarily.

Reserve Requirements: The percentage of certain types of deposits which banks are required to hold at the Fed.

Return on Equity (ROE): A measure of return for each dollar of shareholder investment - in essence, it is how effectively the shareholder's investment is being employed. The percentages can be compared year over year and considered relative to industry composites both to reveal trends and a company's position versus its competitors. ROE is calculated by dividing the annual earnings from operations (see Operating Income) by common shareholders equity (total assets minus total liabilities).

Reverse Repurchase Agreement: A repurchase agreement initiated by the lender of funds. In the case of the Fed, it is the opposite - when the Fed does reverse RPS, it is draining reserves from the banking system. This operation is also referred to as matched-sales.

Rights Offering: An offering of common stock to existing shareholders who hold rights which entitle them to purchase the newly issued shares at a discount to the market price.

ROE: Return on Equity.

ROIC: Return on Invested Capital.

Roll Over: Reinvest funds from a maturing issue into a new issue.

- S -

Selling Short: Selling a security or a futures contract which the seller does not own. It is a strategy used to take advantage of an anticipated decline in price or to protect a long position. In the case of stocks, the seller borrows the stock for delivery, betting that the market price will drop and that the stock can be bought later at a lower price. If a stock is sold short at $20 per share and the price of that stock drops to $15, then the seller can buy the shares at $15, making a profit of $5 per share. Short sellers can face a substantial loss if the stock price rises. They may be forced to buy back the stock at much higher prices then where it was originally sold.

Settlement Date: The date on which a security bought at auction or in the secondary market is delivered in exchange for funds.

Shareholders' Equity: Also called Stockholder's Equity and Net Worth, it is Total Assets minus Total Liabilities of a corporation.

Sovereign Risk: The risks attached to a security when the issuer's country of origin is different from that of the buyer.

Stock Split: Authorized by a company's Board of Directors, splits have the effect of increasing the number of shares outstanding without changing the total market value of the company or diluting a shareholder's percentage stake in the company. The theory behind splits is to lower the stock price so as to make investment in the company available to a broad base on investors. A 2-for-1 split, for example, would give a stockholder of 100 shares trading at $50 per share ownership of 200 shares trading at $25 per share.

Strike Price: Exercise price at which the owner of a call option can purchase the underlying stock or the owner of a put option can sell the underlying stock. The strike price is set by the exchange.

- T -

TED Spread: The difference between Treasury bill and Eurodollar futures prices. A widening TED spread is seen as an indication of credit quality concerns in the banking sector.

Tick: A 1/32nd of a point price move in Treasury prices or bond futures prices.

Ticker Symbol: The abbreviation used to identify a company's securities for trading purposes, such as T for AT&T, and HWP for Hewlett Packard.

TIPS: Treasury Inflation Protected Securities, or CPI-Indexed Treasury Notes.

Total Return: Stocks: The annual increase or decrease in the investment including appreciation, dividends, and interest. The value of a security. Bonds: Held to maturity, it is the Yield to Maturity (see Yield to Maturity). Mutual Funds: The net asset value plus any capital gains and income distribution.

Treasury Bills, Notes, Bonds: Negotiable debt obligations of the U.S. government. *T BILLS* are short-term instruments with maturities of one year or less, issued at a discount from face value. *T NOTES* are intermediate securities with maturities of 1 to 10 years. *T BONDS* are long-term debt instruments with maturities of longer than 10 years.

- U - V -

Undervalued Security: A stock selling below its liquidation value or below the market value that analysts believe it deserves. Undervalued stocks are sought after for investment before the stock price rises and they become fully valued. Undervalued companies are often the target of takeover attempts.

Volume: In the case of the exchanges, it is the total number of stock shares listed on a particular exchange that traded. It is usually measured on a daily basis. The volume of a particular stock, it is the number of shares of that security which traded on a given day.

- W - X - Y - Z -

When-issued: There is a lag between when a Treasury security is announced for sale and when it is actually issued. During this period, the security trades on a when-issued basis, meaning that it trades as if it were issued.

Yankee Bond: A foreign bond issued in the U.S. market and payable in dollars.

Yield Curve: A graph plotting the yields of all bonds of the same quality with maturities ranging from the shortest to the longest available. The resulting curve shows if short-term interest rates are higher or lower than long-term rates. It is used as a tool by analysts to help determine the direction of interest rates. A flat Yield Curve results when there is little difference between short-term and long-term rates. When short-term rates are lower than long-term rates, it is called a positive Yield Curve. Conversely, it is called a negative Yield Curve if short-term rates are higher than long-term rates.

Yield to Maturity (YTM) : The rate of return yielded by a debt security that is held to maturity when both interest payments and the investor's capital gain or loss on the security are taken into account.

APPENDIX:
INVESTMENT POLICY STATEMENT

For

Name

MM/DD/20YY

Investment Objective and Risk Tolerance

The *time horizon* for the Client portfolio is *more than 10 years* before funds may be needed for their purpose.

The primary objective for the portfolio is Growth and Income.

MODERATE: *A Moderate investor values reducing risks and enhancing returns equally. This investor is willing to accept modest risks to seek higher long-term returns. A Moderate investor may endure a short-term loss of principal and lower degree of liquidity in exchange for long-term appreciation.*

Clients' is willing to sacrifice some safety and accept some risk in exchange for higher returns and to stay ahead of inflation. *Client is **not** willing to take above average risk to achieve above average returns. Client can tolerate negative returns from time to time.*

Therefore, a balanced allocation will be employed with a slightly greater allocation to stocks than fixed income to capture growth over a long period of time as described below under "Portfolio Allocations".

Portfolio allocations between stocks and fixed income are an individual decision based on individual circumstances. Work done by Standard & Poor's regarding portfolio allocation using the Efficient Frontier concept of Modern Portfolio Theory, suggests that a portfolio of 60% stocks and 40% Bonds and Fixed Income is the best risk/reward ratio over a long period of time. As a general rule, anyone nearing retirement or depending on their assets for income should not have more than 50% of their portfolio in stocks, and this level may be too high for an individual situation or market environment.

Investment Strategy: Strategic Portfolio Allocation

The strategy employed is considered to be a Strategic Portfolio Allocation Strategy. It is a long term investment strategy where investments are normally held for many years and is not intended to market time and does not chase speculative investments. The investment approach is rooted in the belief that markets are fairly efficient, although not always rational, and that investors' gross returns are determined principally by asset allocation decisions. Strategic asset allocation is compatible with a "buy and hold" strategy; is based on modern portfolio theory, which emphasizes diversification in order to reduce risk and improve portfolio returns.

A Strategic Portfolio Allocation Strategy involves setting target allocations for various asset classes, and periodically rebalancing the portfolio back to the original allocations when they deviate significantly from the initial settings due to differing returns from various assets. In strategic asset allocation, the target allocations depend on a number of factors – such as the investor's risk tolerance, time horizon and investment objectives– and may change over time as these parameters change.

➢ **Stocks** - Stocks have historically had the greatest risk and highest returns among the three major asset categories. As an asset category, stocks are a portfolio's biggest return class, offering the greatest potential for growth. Stocks may achieve big returns but also may produce big losses. The volatility of stocks makes them a very risky investment in the short term.

- ➢ **Bonds** - Bonds are generally less volatile than stocks but offer more modest returns. As a result, an investor approaching a financial goal might increase the allocation to this asset class, because the reduced risk of holding more bonds would be attractive to the investor despite their lower potential for growth. Make note that Bonds carry increased principal risk when interest rates are rising; more on this subject later.

- ➢ **Cash** - Cash and cash equivalents - such as savings deposits, certificates of deposit, treasury bills, money market deposit accounts, and money market funds - are the safest investments, but offer the lowest return of the three major asset categories. The chances of losing money on an investment in this asset category are generally extremely low. The major concern for investors investing in cash equivalents is inflation risk. This is the risk that inflation will outpace and erode investment returns over time.

Portfolio Allocations

Based on client's risk tolerance and timeframe for the investments, the following allocation to stocks and fixed income balances risk and reward appropriately and attempts to achieve the stated objectives of the investment program.

STRATEGIC ALLOCATION STRATEGY:			
	Over-Valued %	**Under-Valued** %	**Mid-Point** %
Risk Assets - Stocks	40%	60%	50%
Fixed Income	60%	40%	50%

When employing a Strategic Allocation, allocations to stocks and fixed income are set within a range depending on the point in the business cycle and the perception of market risk.

- Under normal market conditions, usually based on historic market valuation averages, the allocations will be in the mid-points of the assigned ranges as shown above under the column "Mid-Point".

- When the market is undervalued or after a substantial stock market correction or at the trough of a recession; the expected future return is considered higher at this point in the business cycle. The allocation may be moved to the upper range as noted under the column "Under-valued".

- When the market is significantly over valued based on historic averages, the market risk may be greater at this time and a significant market correction may be likely. This condition usually occurs after a significant market gain and the point in the business cycle is extended. The allocation to stocks may be lowered within the assigned range as noted under the column "Over-valued".

Alternative Strategy:

Investment Strategy: Fixed Allocation

Client prefers a fixed allocation to stocks and fixed income. Therefore, the strategy employed is a Fixed Allocation: The allocation will be maintained regardless of market conditions and will be rebalanced periodically. The portfolio allocations will be reviewed once or twice a year, at the discretion of client, for the purpose of rebalancing.

FIXED ALLOCATION STRATEGY:	
	FIXED %
Risk Assets - Stocks	50%
Fixed Income	50%

DIVERSIFICATION

Stock Allocations

Within the above designated stock allocation for the portfolio; stocks, mutual funds and Exchange Traded funds will be selected that create a well-diversified stock portfolio so that any one company or sector of the market or economy will not on its own dominate the returns of the portfolio.

An emphasis may be placed on funds that have a dividend yield that is equal or better than the general market. This methodology reduces business risk.

International funds will be selected that include a broad cross-section of Europe, the Pacific and possibly some emerging markets.

Certain sectors or global regions may be added from time to time increasing their weighting with the objective to enhance the expected return or mitigate risk.

Stocks and funds will be selected in the following asset categories. *To simplify the sub-allocation, we will view this section as totaling 100% of the stocks in the portfolio.*

Stock Asset Class Category	Range of Allocation	Typical
1. Large Capitalization U.S. Stocks	30-60%	50%
2. Mid-Capitalization U S. Stocks	10-20%	15%
3. Small Capitalization U S. Stocks	5-10%	10%
4. International (non-U.S.) Company Stocks	10-25%	20%
5. Emerging Market Stocks	0-5%	5%
6. Individual Sector over-weighting	0-10%	0%

Fixed Income Allocations

The purpose of this portion of the portfolio is to generate income and reduce overall risk, therefore principal loss is <u>not</u> tolerated.

Bonds tend to rise in value when interest rates fall, and they fall in value when interest rates rise. This is called Interest Rate Risk. Depending on the length of the term of the bonds the resulting movement in principal may be substantial. Therefore the purchase of individual bonds or C.D.'s in a *laddered portfolio* is preferred to mutual funds. This strategy applies to those accounts that allow the purchase of individual securities.

Please see the following topics for more information on these subjects: *Understanding Interest-Rate Risk, Laddered Maturity Portfolio, and Bond Mutual Funds.*

Diversification and Range of Allocations:

The following classes of bonds and C.D.'s would be purchased either individually or through mutual funds or ETFs. See "Asset Quality" section for appropriate ratings.

- <u>U.S. Government Obligations</u>: Treasury bills, notes and bonds, U.S. Agency bonds and FDIC Insured C.D's would be selected depending on which ones provide the best risk/return at the time they are being acquired.

- <u>Corporate Bonds</u>: A mix of investment grade ratings will be selected, as long as the lower end of the investment ratings does not dominate the allocation.

- <u>Municipal Bonds</u>: General Obligation Bonds from *Your Tax State* are preferred, however, other states may be utilized.

- <u>Treasury Inflation Protected Securities (TIPS)</u> may be included as a component of the portfolio for their inflation protection attributes.

- <u>C.D.'s</u>: Federally insured bank deposits by the FDIC.

Fixed income securities or funds will be selected in the following categories. *To simplify the sub-allocation, we will view this section as totaling 100% of the fixed-income portfolio:*

Fixed Income Asset Class Category	Range of Allocation	Typical
1. U.S. Treasury/Agency Bills, Notes, Bonds & C.D.'s	20-80%	30%
2. U.S. Corporate Bonds Investment Grade	20-50%	30%
3. Treasury Inflation Protected Securities	0-20%	10%
4. Municipal Bonds	0-35%	20%
5. Closed-end Bond Funds	0-10%	0%
6. Cash, Money Market, T-bills	5-25%	10%

Understanding Interest-Rate Risk:

Bonds tend to rise in value when interest rates fall, and they fall in value when interest rates rise. Usually, the longer the maturity of the bond, the greater the price volatility will be. This is known as interest rate risk. If an investor holds a bond until maturity, these price fluctuations are of little concern; because at maturity, the investor will receive the par, or face value of the bond.

This inverse relationship between bond prices and interest rates is essentially straightforward as explained below:

- When interest rates rise, new issues come to market with higher yields than older securities, making those older ones worth less. Hence, their prices go down.

- When interest rates decline, new bond issues come to market with lower yields than older securities, making those older, higher-yielding ones worth more. Hence, their prices go up.

- *The "rule of thumb" is that for every 1% of interest rate movement, the principal gain or loss will be the inverse direction equal to the duration of the fund.*

As a result, if a bond must be sold before maturity, it may be worth more or less than originally paid for it, depending on the change in interest rates since the purchase.

Various economic forces affect the level and direction of interest rates in the economy. Interest rates typically climb when the economy is growing, and fall during economic downturns. Similarly, rising inflation leads to rising interest rates (although at some point, higher rates themselves become contributors to higher inflation), and moderating inflation leads to lower interest rates. Inflation is one of the most influential forces on interest rates.

Unusual Economic Cycles:

At certain economic cycles when the yield curve is not normal it may be wise to overweighting either the short term or long term maturities to take advantage of the peculiarity in the yield curve and enhance yield over the long term.

- In a rising rate environment overweighting the shorter term maturities will mitigate interest rate risk and provide the opportunity to reinvest at higher rates. This strategy is very important for bond mutual funds to avoid significant principal loss.
- In a falling rate environment overweighting the longer term maturities will lock in the higher rates and enhance the yield of the portfolio over the long term.

Laddered Maturity Portfolio:

Individual bonds and C.D.'s are purchased with the intention of holding them to maturity. Holding the securities to their maturity is a great way to mitigate the effects of changes in interest rates on the principal of the investment. When the security matures, the face value principal is returned to the investor.

Laddering maturities means dividing the portfolio into years, usually not greater than 10 years. Individual bonds and C.D.'s are purchased, e.g. $1/10^{th}$ of the bonds for year one, $1/10^{th}$ for year two, etc. Then each year 1/10 of the portfolio matures, the face value is paid back and new bonds are purchased at the longest maturity of the ladder.

Laddered portfolios may be built with shorter terms, it is important to pick the appropriate timeframe. If the yield curve does not pay high enough rates at the longer terms, then a shorter ladder, say five years, may be better.

Bond Mutual Funds:

The selection of bond mutual funds is dependent on the point in the economic or business cycle and the length of time before the funds are needed.

- Bond mutual funds are good investments in a <u>stable or falling interest rate</u> environment.
- *Bond mutual funds pool assets and must mark to current market prices daily. The rule of thumb is that for every 1% of interest rate movement, the principal gain or loss will be the inverse direction equal to the duration of the fund.*
- Interest rates rising: To avoid significant principal loss in a rising rate environment, generally funds would be selected with a very short-term duration.
- Criteria: See "Asset Quality", below.

Closed-end Bond Funds:

Closed-end bond funds are funds that have a fixed asset pool and sell usually at a premium or discount to their net asset value. When selling at a discount they may be utilized to enhance the overall yield of the bond portfolio. For a closed-end bond fund to be considered the following criteria must be met:

- The fund is invested in investment grade securities,
- The fund is sold at a substantial discount to its net asset value (NAV),
- The investment manager is a respected bond manager such as PIMCO, Eaton Vance, Black Rock, etc.
- A closed-end fund would be sold when the fund is trading at a premium to net asset value.

ASSET QUALITY

Funds invested herein shall generally conform to the following investment instruments and quality standards. Deviations from these quality standards shall be modest, apply to a small portion of the overall portfolio and explained properly to the Client.

Stocks:

- Equity mutual funds with a Morningstar rating of four or five stars.
- *A Morningstar Rating of three stars is acceptable when funds are not available for the particular market segment at the preferred ratings.*
- Equity Mutual Funds may include Index Funds that track well known and broad indexes, for example, the Standards & Poor's Indexes.
- Investments in broad based index or mutual funds that invest in international regions (i.e., Asia, Europe, Latin America).
- Exchange Traded Funds (ETFs) that track broad based indexes such as the S&P 500 or their sub-indexes.
- Other specialty ETFs that track a particular sector of the stock market for the purpose of over-weighting that sector.
- U. S. Common Stocks: Morningstar and/or Standard & Poor's rating of three to five stars is preferred; a lower rated stock may be selected under certain circumstances. A single stock should not exceed 5% of the portfolio allocation.
- Foreign Stock utilizing the U.S. Depository Receipts (ADR's).

Bonds:

- Bond mutual funds and Exchange Traded Funds with a Morningstar rating of four or five stars; and invested in U.S. Government or investment grade corporate bonds and notes.
- *A Morningstar Rating of three stars is acceptable when funds are not available for the particular market segment at the preferred ratings.*
- U.S. Government bonds, notes and bills.
- U.S. Agency Bonds.
- Corporate bonds and notes with a Standard & Poor's rating of A- or better; or Moody's rating of A3 or better.
- Municipal Bonds: Standard & Poor's rating of AA or better or Moody's equivalent. General obligation bonds are preferred.
- Limit Bond premiums to 5% of par.

Cash: (includes C.D.'s)

- Federally insured bank deposits by the FDIC.
- Money market mutual funds at well-established fund companies invested in assets that predominately comply with the quality provisions stated above.

Rebalancing

Rebalancing is not just a risk-reducing exercise. The goal is to reset the investment mix to bring it back to the expected and appropriate risk level. Sometimes that may mean reducing risk by increasing the portion of a portfolio in the more conservative options; but sometimes it may mean adding more risk to get back to the target mix. That would mean increasing investments in riskier asset classes such as stocks.

The plan for reviewing and rebalancing the portfolios is:

- ✓ Review the portfolio on a quarterly basis.
- ✓ Rebalance the portfolio at least *once a year but twice a year* may be better.

At Rebalancing the allocations will be reviewed to determine new target allocations within the ranges allowed under this policy. The following activities will be considered:

- ✓ *The Point in the Business Cycle*
- ✓ *Any changes in risk tolerance*
- ✓ *Set new target allocations*
- ✓ *Add to Under allocations*
- ✓ *Reduce Over allocations*

When performing the review and rebalancing of the portfolio, a buy/sell sheet will be created. The sell transactions will be entered in the columns under "Sell" and the buy transactions entered in the columns under "Buy".

SELL TRANSACTIONS	ACCOUNT	TKR	Shares	$ AMOUNT		BUY TRANSACTIONS	ACCOUNT	TKR	Shares	$ AMOUNT
		Subtotal						Subtotal		
		Subtotal						Subtotal		
TOTAL SELL TRANSACTIONS . . .						TOTAL BUY TRANSACTIONS . . .				

Name
INVESTMENT POLICY

TARGET ALLOCATIONS
MM/DD/20YY

I. **Stocks Allocation** 50%

Stock Asset Class Category	Allocation %	
1. Large Capitalization U.S. Stocks	50%	
2. Mid-Capitalization U S. Stocks	15%	
3. Small Capitalization U S. Stocks	10%	
4. International (non-U.S.) Company Stocks	20%	
5. Emerging Market Stocks	0%	
6. Individual Sector over-weighting	5%	Total = 100%

II. **Fixed Income Allocation** 50%

Fixed Income Asset Class Category	Allocation %	
1. U.S. Treasury/Agency bills, notes, bonds & C.D.'s	5%	
2. U.S. Corporate Bonds Investment Grade	50%	
3. Treasury Inflation Protected Securities	0%	
4. Municipal Bonds	30%	
5. Closed-end Bond Funds	0%	
6. Cash, Money Market, T-bills	15%	Total = 100%

Maturity Ladder (Limit bond premiums to 5% of par)

0 – 1 Year	20%	
1 – 2 Years	16%	
2 – 3 Years	16%	
3 – 4 Years	16%	
4 – 5 Years	16%	
5 – 6 Years	16%	
6 – 7 Years	0%	
7 – 10 Years	0%	Total = 100%

Ray Gazelle is a Certified Financial Planner™ professional. He is a fee only planner in private practice. Prior to starting his financial planning practice, he enjoyed a career in banking for over 33 years with a large Mid-Atlantic bank. He is active in his community and has offered his services over the years to non-profit organizations as board trustee also serving on their finance committees.

www.ingramcontent.com/pod-product-compliance
Lightning Source LLC
Chambersburg PA
CBHW060042210326
41520CB00009B/1229